M000098359

JOINT LEADERSHIP

LEADING IN A JOINT AND COMBINED MILITARY ORGANIZATION

TED G. ROBERTS

Lieutenant Colonel – US Air Force (retired)

ACKNOWLEDGEMENTS

There are so many people to thank for their help in making this book possible. First, I would like to thank my wife, Ruth, and my three children, Nyla, Alina, and Blake, for their support and patience while I worked on this daunting project. I spent many long hours in the evenings and on weekends going to the local library and reserving a private study room to work on this endeavor.

I started this as my final Doctoral Project for the completion of my Doctorate in Strategic Leadership at Regent University. The genesis for the idea for this book came from a good friend and mentor, Doctor Fred Kienle, Colonel-US Army retired. He suggested that I should write about and develop an elective course for the Joint Forces Staff College (JFSC) in "Joint Leadership." While the JFSC has done a great job for many years in teaching students of all military branches about how the Department of Defense works and how to perform Joint Planning, there really isn't much time in the curriculum devoted to how to lead officers from other services in a Joint (multi-service) or Combined (multi-national) organization. My own personal experiences showed that most of my supervisors from other branches did not have a good understanding of Air Force appraisal systems, and most officers have to learn through a "trial by fire" when it comes to rating subordinates from other services. Unwritten rules that apply for rating Air Force officers don't work when rating on Soldiers, Sailors, Marines, and Guardians, and vice versa. My colleagues who allowed me to interview them and gain their insights on their respective services' rating systems were invaluable to this project, and I sincerely thank them for their time, insights, and permission to quote them in this book.

I also thank my Doctoral Project Chair, Doctor Virginia Richardson. She was a tremendous help guiding me through the process of completing this manuscript. She provided a great process for how to develop this book and write it to an appropriate audience. My additional reader, Doctor Gary Oster, also was a strong advocate for my writing and I learned a lot from him as a mentor and professor. Unfortunately, we lost him in 2021, and all the Regent DSL Program students who had the opportunity to meet him most definitely miss him. I also thank Doctors Kathleen Patterson, DSL Program Director and Doris Gomez, Dean of the School of Business and Leadership, who were great influences and mentors throughout my time in the Regent DSL program.

Finally, I would like to dedicate this book to the memory of my dad, Grover C. Roberts. He was my greatest champion growing up and an ideal father figure.

TABLE OF CONTENTS

INTRODUCTION

You receive the email from your service's officer assignment team with the phrase "Official Assignment Notification" in the subject line. You open the message and see you've been assigned to a "Joint organization." Like all military officers from any of the five military services, you've excelled at your tactical level assignments for ten or more years. Now you face the opportunity to leave your traditional service organizations and serve in a Joint Duty Assignment List (JDAL) billet in a joint headquarters. This assignment means you'll move to a base that is very likely run by a different military service, and you will undoubtedly have to work with and potentially lead officers from other services. What are the service cultures that they bring? What joint organizational differences will you need to learn? How will you survive and even succeed in this new joint or combined environment? Some of what worked for you throughout your previous years of service will continue to work well in a joint organization. However, you will likely need to tailor your leadership skills and even cultivate new ones to succeed in this new environment. This book seeks to help officers assigned to their first joint assignment to flourish and grow in this exciting new environment, and also to avoid some of the pitfalls that other officers have experienced in the past.

Ideally, officers assigned to a joint organization will attend the ten-week Joint Professional Military Education Level II (JPME II) class either enroute to the joint assignment or within their first year in the assignment. Unfortunately, most officers report into their joint assignment and either attend JPME II near the end of their assignment, or they never get to attend and must find the time and get their service to nominate them late in their careers. Some officers get JPME II credit by attending their senior level education (i.e. service war colleges), but the war colleges only devote time in their curriculum to joint education as mandated by law (10 USC-107) and Department of Defense policy (CJCSI 1800.01F). While officers may receive a quick overview of the joint strategy-making methods and the joint planning process, they don't receive the in-depth education they would receive by attending the ten-week course. Even officers attending the ten-week residence course in Norfolk receive an education that focuses on the strategy and planning side. Still, JPME allocates limited time for learning joint leadership or understanding the rating systems on officers from other services outside of informal conversations that may take place after hours between students from the different services.

First, what is a Joint Organization? A joint organization is any department of defense combatant command headquarters, Joint Staff, or other agency that has military officers from at least two different services working there. While the Army and Air Force have Major Commands and the Navy has Fleet Commands, these service commands typically only have officers from those respective services present. By contrast, a joint command like U.S. Central Command, U.S. Indo-Pacific Command, U.S. European Command, and others will often have more than a thousand military officers working from all the services. Officers can also find themselves assigned to a Joint Task Force (JTF) or even a Combined Task Force (CTF). Combined organizations will include officers from other nations in addition to officers from all the services. Arriving as a new member of one of these Joint or Combined organizations can feel intimidating and exciting at the same time. This assignment also presents a tremendous opportunity to work with and lead officers from other services or nations, but even more to learn from them and gain insight into their knowl-edge, experiences, and perspectives.

Second, what is a JDAL billet? The Goldwater-Nichols Act of 1986 mandated that the services develop Joint Qualified Officers (JQOs) to ensure joint perspectives in senior leaders. Earning designation by your service as a Joint Qualified Officer requires two actions. First, an officer must complete the required 36 months in a joint assignment as defined by Goldwater-Nichols.

Joint organizations designate officer billets in the O4 (Major or Lieutenant Commander) through O6 (Colonel or Captain) as JDAL billets. Officers who fill these billets earn joint credit during their time in the organization. Second, the officer must earn Joint Professional Military Education Level II (JPME II) credit. The most common way officers complete JPME II is by attending the ten-week course at the Joint and Combined Warfighting School (JCWS) in Norfolk. However, officers can also earn JPME II equivalency credit by attending a senior service school such as the National War College, Eisenhower School, or any of the services' War Colleges (Army, Naval, Air, or Marine War College). Once an officer has completed both requirements, 36 months in a JDAL billet plus JPME II, their service will designate them as a Joint Qualified Officer (JQO).

Finally, this book will serve as a navigation tool to help officers navigate the waters of working in a joint organization. It will help shed light on some of the respective service cultures, offer a glimpse of multi-service perspectives, provide an understanding about combatant commands, the Joint Staff, and understanding organizations that are joint and combined. The reader will gain insight into the design of these joint organizations, the interactions between them, and how the joint, interagency, intergovernmental, and multinational (JIIM) environments differ from service headquarters organizations. An officer heading to their first joint assignment should be able to gain a robust initial understanding of the joint environment and also can use this book a valuable reference to help them survive and thrive in their joint assignment. The reader likely has an extensive "bottom-up" view of how tactics support operational-level plans and strategic-level policies. This book will give the reader a "top-down" perspective of national strategies, theater strategies, and how those go into guiding Combatant Commanders and their staffs to create operational-level plans. The reader will gain insight into the Joint Planning Process (JPP), which can prove particularly challenging for officers who have never conducted military planning nor have exposure to the joint planning and other service planning processes.

The reader will also gain valuable insight into the other services' officer personnel systems and performance appraisal systems. How does an Army

Officer Evaluation Report (OER) differ from an Air Force Officer Performance Report, a Marine Officer's Fitness Report (FITREP), and a Navy Officer's FITREP? All the services have evolved very different formats for conducting annual appraisals on their personnel, and there is no training course available that offers the officer transitioning to a joint assignment the necessary insight into how to complete these forms for officers from other services, what references to read, or what unwritten rules apply. I hope that an officer assigned to work in and lead others in a joint or combined organization can read this work and gain an excellent working knowledge of what they will face in a joint or combined organization. This knowledge will help this officer avoid the pitfalls, overcome some of the stereotypes and preconceived notions, and arrive at their assignment ready to learn rapidly, represent their respective service well, and contribute significantly to the joint mission. Ultimately, following the successful completion of their joint tour and return to their respective service, this officer will have attained a much broader perspective of where their service fits in, and this perspective will make them much more effective commanders and mentors to their people when they return to their service.

CHAPTER 1:

What Are Joint and Combined

"Separate ground, sea, and air warfare is gone forever. If ever we should be involved in war, we will fight in all elements, with all services, as one single concentrated effort."

— *General of the Army Dwight D. Eisenhower*

Throughout our nation's history, we have engaged in "joint" operations to varying degrees. Even Washington's victory at Yorktown in 1781 that secured American victory over the British in the Revolutionary War required coordination between Army and Naval forces. As the nation and warfare evolved, the Army and Navy increased their joint cooperation. Following the poor joint military operations in the 1898 Spanish-American War, the Secretary of War and the Secretary of the Navy established the Joint Army and Navy Board in 1903.[1] World War II brought an increased focus on "jointness" as the Joint Board expanded to six members. However, this iteration of the Joint Board had minimal legal authority and was disbanded in 1947.

The National Security Act of 1947 implemented the most sweeping reforms of the U.S. military to that point. This act established the National Security Council (NSC), established the Department of Defense, created the United States Air Force as a separate but equal service, and made the Departments of the Army, Navy, and Air Force subordinate to the Department of Defense.

This act also established the Joint Chiefs of Staff and created the position of the Chairman of the Joint Chiefs of Staff as the senior military officer and principal military advisor to the President. Despite these reforms, interservice rivalries and competition for budgets continued to plague the military throughout the next 40 years. The 1986 Goldwater-Nichols Act sought to change that with another round of significant reforms.

Congress passed the 1986 Goldwater-Nichols Act to reform the Department of Defense and begins with the following purpose:

> "To reorganize the Department of Defense and strengthen civilian authority in the Department of Defense, to improve the military advice to the President, the National Security Council, and the Secretary of Defense, to place clear responsibility on the commanders of the unified and specified combatant commands for the accomplishment of missions assigned to those commands and ensure that the authority of those commanders is fully commensurate with that responsibility, to provide for more efficient use of defense resources, to improve joint officer management policies, otherwise to enhance the effectiveness of military operations and improve the management and administration of the Department of Defense" (Goldwater-Nichols Act, 1986).[2]

Key provisions in the Goldwater-Nichols Act included a requirement for joint officer management, including the requirement for the Secretary of Defense to track promotion rates for "officers who are serving in, or have served in, joint duty assignments."[3] The Goldwater-Nichols Act also directed that joint duty assignments shall not be less than three years. Additionally, the Act stated that "an officer may not be selected for promotion to the grade of brigadier general or rear admiral (lower half) unless the officer has served in a joint duty assignment."[4] These clauses in the legislation clearly spell out the importance of joint duty in an officer's career. The Secretary of Defense has a mandate from Congress to track and report on joint officer management, and joint duty experience is a legislative prerequisite for promotion to the most senior levels in the military.

Joint Duty typically requires working in the Joint, Interagency, Intergovernmental, and Multinational (JIIM) environments. The U.S. Code defines Joint Duty as "limited to assignments to assignments in which (i) the preponderance of duties of the officer involve joint matters and (ii) the officer gains significant experience in joint matters."[5] Joint organizations include the Joint Staff in the Pentagon or assignment to the staff of any one of the eleven geographic or functional combatant command headquarters. The six geographic combatant commands include U.S. Indo-Pacific Command, European Command, Africa Command, Northern Command, or Southern Command. Functional combatant commands include U.S. Transportation Command, Strategic Command, Special Operations Command, Space Command, and Cyber Command.[6] Assignment to any of these commands will mean working alongside and leading officers from multiple services. Additionally, these assignments will include coordinating with other U.S. Government agencies like the State Department, Treasury Department, and the Department of Homeland Security to name a few. Intergovernmental means working with government employees from partner nations as well as Intergovernmental organizations (IGOs) like the United Nations, the North Atlantic Treaty Organization (NATO), and the African Union (AU). Finally, officers working in a Multinational environment will find themselves working in a "Combined" (i.e., multinational) headquarters or Combined Joint Task Force (CJTF). Officers assigned to U.S. Forces Korea (USFK) or U.S. Forces Japan (USFJ) will quickly find they have daily interactions with Korean or Japanese officer counterparts who work in the headquarters in addition to working with members of all of the other U.S. military services.

Today's "Armed Forces of the United States consist of six military Services—the Army, Marine Corps, Navy, Air Force, Space Force, and Coast Guard.[7] The President signed the Fiscal Year 2020 (FY20) National Defense Authorization Act on December 20, 2019, which formally established the newest military service, the United States Space Force. This latest reform represented the most monumental change in the U.S. military organizational structure since the 1947 National Security Act separated the Air Corps from the Department of the Army and established the United States Air Force as a separate service. The

FY20 NDAA "recognizes space as a warfighting domain" on par with air, land, and sea, and "establishes the U.S. Space Force in Title 10 as the sixth Armed Service of the United States, under the U.S. Air Force."[8] Initially, the Space Force will consist primarily of Air Force personnel assigned to space career fields. Over the next two years, these personnel, as well as some space personnel from the Army and Navy, will transition to comprise the U.S. Space Force.

The days when a particular service goes to war alone have long since passed. In today's conflicts, "the nation goes to war, using all its Services' capabilities in the combination that best suits the particular threat posed and the war plan designed to defeat it."[9] The terms "Joint" and "Jointness" have grown to mean any cooperative effort that includes personnel and capabilities from more than one of these military Services. Each of the services possesses and develops core competencies in their respective warfighting domains. The Army, Navy, and Air Force pride themselves on maintaining excellence on land, on the sea, or in the air. The U.S. Space Force will build on its core competency to operate in the formally declared space domain. However, the word *joint* has evolved to be "used in a variety of contexts."[10] *Joint* can refer to particular organizations like the Joint Staff and Combatant Command headquarters, it can depict "the strategic and operational responsibilities" of those headquarters, and it often describes the interoperability of the forces and equipment of the different services.[11]

Increasingly, "joint" headquarters also include personnel from and coordinate their efforts with other entities outside the Department of Defense. Combatant Command and Joint Task Force (JTF) headquarters organizations frequently have representatives from other U.S. Government agencies such as the FBI, CIA, State Department, the U.S. Agency for International Development (USAID), the Department of Homeland Security (DHS), Treasury Department, and other agencies. Military officers assigned to "joint duty" may even find themselves working in these other government agencies as liaisons. CJTF-76 in Afghanistan in 2006 had representatives from the FBI, USAID, and also the U.S. Department of Agriculture. The Department of Agriculture representative taught classes to Afghanistan government officials and farmers on how to grow crops, crop rotation, soil analysis, and other agricultural topics relevant to helping Afghanistan farmers improve food production. With the help of U.S. military space personnel, the Department of Agriculture representative was able to link up with The National-Geospatial Intelligence Agency (NGA) representatives to acquire space-based imagery and maps that he was able to use to teach Afghan farmers about soil moisture content analysis that they could use to improve crop yields.[12] This anecdote represents the power of joint and interagency coordination to solve problems and improve conditions in any environment.

The core document that defines the organization of the joint warfighting community is the Unified Command Plan (UCP). Signed by the President, this document establishes the Combatant Commands (i.e., joint commands), defines their geographic or functional area of responsibility, and may also designate specific responsibilities. U.S. Northern Command (USNORTHCOM), headquartered on Peterson Air Force Base in Colorado Springs, is responsible for the North American continent and the adjoining waters, including the Gulf of Mexico. With this area of responsibility, USNORTHCOM operates in the United States and has responsibilities to coordinate and operate with civil authorities, and particularly to perform "Defense Support of Civil Authorities (DSCA), at the U.S. federal, tribal, state, and local levels."[13] This requirement to operate within U.S. borders and coordinate closely with agencies such as the FBI, state, and local authorities make USNORTHCOM unique among the Combatant Commands. All the other commands either operate in areas of responsibility outside the U.S. borders, or they act in a functional way such as United States Transportation Command, Special Operations Command, or Space Command.

Some Combatant Commands must also work with Intergovernmental organizations. U.S. European Command has the European continent and surrounding waters defining its area of responsibility. However, U.S. forces operating in this area also function as part of the North Atlantic Treaty Organization (NATO). NATO has its intergovernmental headquarters in Belgium with other sub-headquarters in the United Kingdom and Norfolk, Virginia. U.S. officers may find themselves assigned to joint duty at U.S. European

Command headquarters and will likely engage with NATO as part of their regular duties. Officers may also work in the NATO headquarters assigned as NATO staff officers. This environment will differ significantly from duty at a U.S. command headquarters. Officers will immediately work with offers from the 29 NATO member nations like France, Germany, Greece, Portugal, the United Kingdom, or others.[14]

Finally, officers frequently find themselves working in multinational organizations or multinational forces. Multi-National Force Iraq (MNF-I) represents a relatively recent example. Any time United States military personnel find themselves working in a Combined/Joint Task Force (CJTF) comprised of military forces from two or more nations, they have entered a multi-national setting. Combined Joint Task Force for Operation INHERENT RESOLVE (CJTF-OIR), established in 2014, emerged as a multinational organization. While led by a U.S. Army general, the Deputy Commanding General of CJTF-OIR was a British Army officer, and officers from Australia and other nations soon filled key staff positions throughout the headquarters. This transformation of Army Central Command (ARCENT) Headquarters into a Joint and, ultimately, a Combined/Joint organization brought interesting cultural dynamics. Today, CJTF-OIR still has a staff of 500 personnel and boasts the motto "One mission, many nations."[15] OIR grew to include contributions from more than sixty Coalition partners at its peak.[16]

Working in these Joint or Combined organizations will present many opportunities and challenges for officers. Officers accustomed to common language using service-specific lexicon will likely have to adjust their thinking and communication style to accommodate working with officers from other services. Even common military language may not translate when officers must work with U.S. civilians from other government agencies, and working with people from other nations will require additional tact and understanding. People from other agencies and partner nations bring unique perspectives and add significant capabilities to the joint or combined organization. They bring to bear other instruments of national power such as diplomacy, information, or economic capabilities that contribute tremendously to fulfilling interests for both the United States and allied nations. Officers will gain much cultural expertise and broaden their perspective on how the U.S. achieves its strategic goals that will serve them well after their joint tour when they return to their respective services.

1   Joint Forces Staff College, *Student Text 1, The Joint Staff Officer's Guide,* (Norfolk, VA: National Defense University, 2019), 1-3.

2   *Goldwater-Nichols Department of Defense Reorganization Act of 1986,* HR 3622, 99th Cong. (1 October 1986): Public Law 99–433, 2.

3   *Goldwater-Nichols Act,* 38.

4   *Goldwater-Nichols Act,* 38.

5   10 U.S. Code, Chapter 38, 668(b)(1).

6   Department of Defense. *Combatant Commands.* Accessed November 15, 2019. https://www.defense.gov/Our-Story/Combatant-Commands.

7   R.M. Swain and A. C. Pierce (Eds.) "Service Identity and Joint Warfighting," *The Armed Forces Officer,* (Washington DC: NDU Press, 2017), 129–144.

8   FY2020 NDAA Summary of the National Defense Authorization Act of Fiscal Year 2020, SR 1790, 116th Cong. (20 December 2019): Public Law 116–92, 14.

9   Swain and Pierce, "Service Identity," 129–144.

10   D. Robert Worley. "Shaping U.S. Military Forces: Revolution or Relevance in a Post-Cold War World." (Westport, CT: Praeger Security International, 2006), 11.

11   D. Robert Worley. "Shaping U.S. Military Forces," 11.

12   Theodore G. Roberts personal experience in Afghanistan 2006-2007.

13   Joint Forces Staff College, *Student Text 1,* 7–34.

14   North Atlantic Treaty Organization (NATO). https://www.nato.int/cps/en/natolive/nato_countries.htm

15   Combined Joint Task Force Operation Inherent Resolve, *About,* https://www.inherentresolve.mil/About-CJTF-OIR/Coalition/.

16   Combined Joint Task Force Operation Inherent Resolve, *History.* Headquarters CJTF-OIR, 17 October—31 July 2017, 1–2. https://www.inherentresolve.mil/Portals/14/Documents/Mission/HISTORY_17OCT2014-JUL2017.pdf?ver=2017-07-22-095806-793

CHAPTER 2:
Service Cultures in a Joint Organization

Officers assigned to a joint or combined organization will have to accommodate organizational cultures on multiple levels. Edgar Schein identified four categories of culture.

Figure 1: Categories of Culture

Culture	Category
Macrocultures	Nations, ethnic and religious groups, occupations that exist globally
Organizational cultures	Private, public, nonprofit, government organizations
Subcultures	Occupational groups within organizations
Microcultures	Microsystems within or outside organizations

Source: Edgar Schein. "Organizational Culture and Leadership, 4th Ed.

Most combatant command headquarters will primarily be joint organizations; however, they will also have coalition officers assigned to them as liaison officers from partner nations. U.S. European Command headquarters, located in Stuttgart, Germany, will have German military officers present. These officers from different countries will expose U.S. officers to macrocultures based on nationalities. Additionally, the military profession exists globally, so while macrocultures based on nationality may present barriers, the macroculture based on the common military profession will make it easier to connect and work with officers from other nations.

Perhaps the biggest culture shock for a newly assigned officer arriving at her joint assignment will center around organizational cultures. After spending ten years or more working almost exclusively in service (e.g., Air Force, Army, Navy) organizations, the officer must learn to understand, work with, and lead officers from other services while respecting their service cultures. Each military service has its own strong yet unique culture that has evolved over decades or even centuries of history. While U.S. officers will share a common macroculture based on mutual nationality, these officers will each bring their own unique organizational service culture rooted in the traditions and histories of their respective services. Additionally, each service contains subcultures associated with career fields within that service. Air Force officers can come from the pilot (rated operations) community; space, intelligence, air battle manager, and cyber communities (nonrated operations); or non-operational career fields such as personnel, finance, legal, or medical career fields. Each service has similar subcultures based on functional areas.

United States Army

The United States Army is the senior service, established first in 1775. The Army has a strong organizational culture that has evolved over its 244-year history. Names of great historical figures like General George Washington, Ulysses S. Grant, John Pershing, Douglas MacArthur, George Marshall, Dwight Eisenhower, Norman Schwarzkopf, and Colin Powell have formed the culture and ethos of the United States Army. Army officers have great pride in their Service and view their branch as the "senior service." This fact is embodied daily with every Joint Service Color Team that places the Department of the Army flag as the rightmost flag next to the U.S. flag. The Army's mission statement emphasizes the Service's focus on land dominance as part of the joint force.

> **"The Army Mission – our purpose – remains constant: To deploy, fight and win our nation's wars by providing ready, prompt and sustained land dominance by Army forces across the full spectrum**

of conflict as part of the joint force. The Army mission is vital to the nation because we are the service capable of defeating enemy ground forces and indefinitely seizing and controlling those things an adversary prizes most – its land, its resources and its population." [1]

Army officers learn at the earliest point in their careers the importance of detailed planning using the Military Decision-Making Process (MDMP). The Army emphasizes individual and small group leadership at the earliest point in their careers when new Army Lieutenants serve as platoon leaders in charge of 20–40 enlisted soldiers. By the time they reach captain, Army officers lead companies consisting of as many as 200 soldiers. As a result, by the time Army officers reach senior levels, they have extensive leadership and planning expertise that the Army has drilled into them at the core cultural level. As a result, Army officers often arrive at joint assignments as very adept planners based on their extensive planning experience.

The Army is the largest service with over 500,000 soldiers. General George Casey, the Army's Chief of Staff from 2007-11, stated that "three traits—*vision, courage,* and *character*—will form the essence of effective military leaders in the years ahead"[2] The Army places a strong emphasis on building character, and it accomplishes this by instilling the Seven Army Values from day one—Loyalty, Duty, Respect, Selfless Service, Honor, Integrity, and Personal Courage—values that Army holds form the basis for morally strong and ethical Soldiers and leaders.[3] Within this Army macroculture, reside several strong subcultures. Most Army officers identify with their combat arms specialties such as Infantry, Artillery, or Armor, and with this comes a strong sense of belonging to a sub-organization with its own unique history, tradition, and artifacts.

While the Army possesses a strong organizational culture grounded in 240 years of tradition, it also has strong subcultures among its combat arms divisions. Soldiers typically work in either the Infantry, Armor, Artillery, or Aviation units. Each of these career fields within the Army has developed a strong subculture within the Army, and often rivalries between these sub-organizations influence how the Army operates and prioritizes its resources. These subcultures also heavily influence who advances and leads in the Army, and therefore who holds command during military operations. Dr. James M. Smith stated, "The Army organizational essence is defined in clear terms of ground combat. The infantry is the 'Queen of Battle,' artillery is the 'King,' and armor (the 'Prince'?) is also a traditional member of the core combat 'elite.'"[4]

United States Marine Corps

The U.S. Marine Corps is the United States' second oldest service. According to former Marine Corps Commandant, General James T. Conway, "Marines and their officers *are* different," and this difference "starts with the Corps' culture."[5] One key reason stems from the Marine Corps' focus on every Marine as a rifle-man first. General Conway cites four reasons why Marine officers are different from their peers in other services. First, every officer, regardless of specialty, begins their career with six months learning how to command a rifle platoon.[6] This method inculcates a deep sense of belonging to the Corps and its organizational culture first, and places subcultures in a secondary position. Second, all Marine officers view their primary purpose as "to enable, support, or lead grim-faced 19-year-old Lance Corporals."[7] Third, Marine officers hold a strong sense of and loyalty to the Corps' history and view it as their personal responsibility to maintain the legacy of their unit. Finally, Marine officers feel confident that they will have to deploy to some austere location on the earth where they will have to lead their unit "to adapt and overcome both the environment and the enemy."[8] These facets of Marine culture readily emerge through the Marine Corps' mission statement.

> **"As America's expeditionary force in readiness since 1775, the U.S. Marines are forward deployed to win our Nation's battles swiftly and aggressively in times of crisis. We fight on land, sea and air, as well as provide forces and detachments to naval ships and ground operations."** [9]

The Marine Corps is also the United States' smallest service, with only 180,000 members. The Corps has a very strong organizational culture steeped in over two centuries of history and tradition. The Marine Corps song, that Marines sing at many events, contains words that harken back to its earliest exploits. "From the Halls of Montezuma, to the shores of Tripoli" reminds Marines that they trace their history to the earliest battles of the country. "The Halls of Montezuma refers to the Battle of Chapultapec in 1847 that Marines fought during the Mexican-American War.[10] According to the Marine Corps website, the Marines "stormed the enemy fortress" to capture Palacio Nacional and disrupt the Mexican army.[11] After two days, the "Marines gained control of the castle, better known as the "Halls of Montezuma."[12] "To the shores of Tripoli" evokes memories of the Marines fighting the pirates that had been raiding American merchant ships off the Barbary Coast. President Thomas Jefferson dispatched the Marines to fight back.[13] Lieutenant Presley O'Bannon led his Marines on a 600-mile march across the Libyan Desert to storm the Tripolitan city of Derna and rescue the kidnapped crew of the USS *Philadelphia*.[14] In honor of his victory, the Ottoman Empire Viceroy, Prince Hamet, presented Lieutenant O'Bannon with a Mameluke sword. This classic artifact is the model for the ceremonial sword Marines wear today.[15]

Marines take great pride in their strong history and Marine Corps culture. They call themselves "trained to improvise, adapt, and overcome any obstacle in whatever situation they are needed" and will engage "until victory is seized."[16] Heroes like Lieutenant General Lewis B. "Chesty" Puller, who joined the Marines in World War I, fought valiantly while leading Marines at Guadalcanal in World War II, and continued with the fighting withdrawal against the Chinese at the Chosin Reservoir in the Korean War.[17] Other Marines who epitomize their legend include Colonel Pappy Boyington, General Anthony Zinni, and General James Mattis. Marines are incredibly adept staff officers and typically bring a great attitude and add tremendously to the joint and combined organizations in which they serve.

Similar to Army officers, Marines employ the Marine Corps Planning Process (MCPP) at the earliest points in their officer careers. They build extensive experience conducting planning at the tactical unit level and know how to perform Mission Analysis, develop an approach, and craft courses of action. This background serves Marine officers well when they arrive on a joint staff and have to participate in a planning effort using the Joint Planning Process.

United States Navy

While technically the United States' third oldest service, the United States Navy has always viewed itself as a co-equal branch of the Army. Since 1789, the United States had two departments, the Department of War and the Department of the Navy. After 1947, the Department of the Navy made up about one-third of the Department of Defense. Navy culture has evolved "around combat ships designed to control the seas."[18] While junior Navy officers serve in positions with limited autonomy on their ship, they observe their senior officers, the ship captains, commanding their ships far from shore with almost complete independence. As a result, by the time naval officers serve in a joint assignment, they have developed a fierce sense of independence, and highly value sea service above shore duty or even joint assignments.[19] With this organizational culture, the US Navy has the following mission.

> **"The mission of the Navy is to recruit, train, equip, and organize to deliver combat-ready Naval forces to win conflicts and wars while maintaining security and deterrence through sustained forward naval presence."** [20]

Like the Army, the Navy has an internal competition between subcultures. The surface Navy (Surface Warfare Officers or SWOs) has the longest tradition dating back to the Navy's earliest days characterized by battles of fleets comprised of battleships, cruisers, and frigates.[21] The Submariners (pronounced SUB-mar-een-ers, not sub-MARE-in-ers) gained influence across the nuclear age as the Navy began powering their ships with nuclear reactors replacing diesel engines. The Aviators and carrier advocates today dominate the Navy with their tremendous influence that grew from World War II as the aircraft carrier replaced the battleships as the preeminent representation of naval sea power.

The aircraft carriers are the largest ships in the fleet, and other surface warfare ships frequently sail with the carriers as part of Carrier Strike Groups (CSGs) with the role of supporting and protecting the carrier. Despite being the largest surface ships in the fleet, carriers are essentially mobile airports and always sail with an aviator, not a surface warfare officer in command.

Most Navy officers will readily tell you that while they have a planning process in the Navy, the Navy Planning Process (NPP), most of them have minimal planning expertise when they arrive on a joint staff. Some will even joke that "Plan" is a four-letter word in the Navy. Typically, Navy officers on the Navy component staff will conduct planning for the Carrier Strike Groups, and these plans then go to the ships to employ the plan. Surface Warfare Officers will drive their ships appropriately, and aviators will do day-to-day mission planning for the aircraft, but by and large, officers on the ships do not engage in planning using the NPP.[22] While this may present challenges when serving on a joint planning group and learning the joint planning processes, Naval officers do very well on joint staffs and apply well-ingrained attention to detail they have cultivated throughout their maritime careers.

United States Air Force

Until December 2020, the United States Air Force was the newest military service. Emerging from the U.S. Army's Signal Corps in the early twentieth century, the earliest officers were brave men like Henry "Hap" Arnold, Claire Chenault, and Carl Spaatz. The initial Army pilots like Hap Arnold received their flying training by attending schools run by the Wright Brothers in Dayton, Ohio.[23] The earliest vision for airpower in the military viewed aircraft solely as aerial observation platforms. However, World War I saw the emergence of aircraft as a means to attack ground targets and even saw the first aerial dogfights. Throughout the interwar years, Army aviation continued to evolve and grow. By the time World War II started, Hap Arnold had risen to become the Commander of the Army Air Forces, and airpower played a vital role in the Allied victory in World War II, both in the European Theater of Operations and in the Pacific.

Recognizing how the air had become a domain on par with land and sea, Congress passed the National Security Act of 1947 which disbanded the Department of the War and the Navy, established a Department of Defense, and created the Department of the Air Force as an equal branch of service with the Army and Navy. While the Air Force emerged from the Army with some of the Army's organizational cultural influence, it evolved its own unique organizational culture based on an aviation mindset of bold action and innovation. The Air Force's mission statement captures this mindset to fly, fight, and win but also recognizes two additional warfighting domains that have emerged over the last few decades – space and cyberspace. The Air Force has clearly led the Department of Defense in space with a major command, Air Force Space Command, established in the early 1980s and focused on operating in space and delivering space-based effects.

"The mission of the United States Air Force is to fly, fight, and win in air, space, and cyberspace."[24]

Like the Army and Navy, the Air Force has subcultures within its ranks and a hierarchy of who leads. Officers go into rated operations (pilots and navigators), non-rated operations (Space, Missiles, Intelligence, and Cyberspace Operations), and other supporting career fields. As expected, pilots dominate the Air Force as most of the top generals in the Air Force are and have always been rated pilots. Only pilots have ever held the top position of Chief of Staff of the Air Force, and the preponderance of the Air Force's top generals wear command pilot wings. Even within the Air Force's flying communities, a hierarchy has emerged between the fighter pilots, air mobility pilots, bomber pilots, and helicopter pilots. Fighter pilots have dominated the Air Force hierarchy for many decades, and most of the Air Force Chiefs of Staff grew out of the fight pilot subculture.

Air Force officers will have varied planning experience depending on their career field and background. Space officers will have a global viewpoint based on their space perspective, working with satellites and global space systems that orbit the earth. Pilots often have strong planning experience due to the requirements to conduct detailed mission planning for aircraft sorties. The Air Force also ingrains the debrief process into its pilots and other operational career fields. This deep introspective process forces operators to conduct detailed mission planning, execute their mission, and then conduct a detailed after-action analysis known as the Debrief. The debrief process seeks to identify strengths and weaknesses and develop robust Lessons Learned that can improve future missions and share those lessons across the operational community. This experience makes many Air Force officers also effective planners when they arrive in a joint organization.

Bold pilots like Chuck Yeager, Robin Olds, Buzz Aldrin form the ethos of the Air Force and serve as its cultural icons. Chuck Yeager served as a fighter pilot and test pilot, and he famously became the first to break the sound barrier in the skies over Edwards Air Force Base. Brigadier General Robin Olds graduated from West Point in 1942. However, he went to pilot training, flew over the D-Day invasion force at Normandy, and became an ace in World War II. He continued to serve for 30 years, including as a Wing Commander and F-4 pilot during the Vietnam War, and almost earned ace status again in that war. Around the same time Robin Olds flew his last combat mission in Vietnam, Lieutenant Buzz Aldrin joined Neil Armstrong on the Apollo 11 mission in becoming the first humans to walk on the moon. The commonality in all three of these stories ties to the Air Force's focus as a future-oriented organization closely related to developing and using the most advanced technologies.[25]

United States Space Force

Space is the most dynamic warfighting domain, with many countries claiming to be space-faring nations. The U.S. Department of Defense has undergone significant changes with its operations in the space domain over the last 40 years. The Air Force established Air Force Space Command and headquartered it at Peterson Air Force Base in Colorado in 1982.[26] Air Force Space Command's mission is to "Provide resilient and affordable space capabilities for the Air Force, Joint Force and the Nation."[27] The President signed the order in 2018, establishing a joint command, U.S. Space Command, as a warfighting command for space equivalent to other regional commands like U.S. European Command, Central Command, and Indo-Pacific Command. Whereas Air Force Space Command served as a component of the Air Force to organize, train, and equip space forces, U.S. Space Command focused on the warfighting aspect and employing those forces with the following mission:

> "The USSPACECOM mission is to deter aggression and conflict, defend U.S. and allied freedom of action, deliver space combat power for the Joint/Combined force, and develop joint warfighters to advance U.S. and allied interests in, from, and through the space domain." [28]

The Space Commission of 2001 and other entities have long called for the establishment of a separate space service focused on space, however; and criticized the Air Force for subordinating the space career field to the flying community. The National Defense Authorization Act of 2020, signed into law on December 20, 2019, formally established a separate U.S. Space Force within the Department of the Air Force. The U.S. Space Force performs the following mission.

> **The U.S. Space Force is a military service that organizes, trains, and equips space forces in order to protect U.S. and allied interests in space and to provide space capabilities to the joint force. USSF responsibilities will include developing military space professionals, acquiring military space systems, maturing the military doctrine for space power, and organizing space forces to present to our Combatant Commands.** [29]

This mission statement clearly identifies the Space Force's role as organizing, training, and equipping space forces for the joint force (e.g., U.S. Space Command), but adds language dedicated explicitly to developing space professionals. While born out of the U.S. Air Force, the Space Force will evolve its own organizational culture in the years ahead, similar to how the Air Force emerged from and grew out of its genesis as part of the Army.

Joint Acculturation

Can a joint culture emerge over the presence of these service cultures? Bringing officers together from these services to work on common joint problems certainly lends itself to these individuals growing accustomed to each other and learning about their sister services. The Goldwater-Nichols Act levies a requirement on officers to complete Joint Professional Military Education via a resident course to attain Joint Qualified Officer (JQO) status. They primarily accomplish this by attending the Joint Forces Staff College's ten-week Joint Professional Military Education II (JPME II) course. A major aspect of this course, outside of the knowledge gained about the joint community and joint processes, involves joint officer acculturation. Approximately 180 students from all services and each combatant command and the joint staff descend on the campus in Norfolk, Virginia, to learn about jointness and joint operations. The school divides these students into seminars of 16–18 people with a broad mix of Army, Marine, Navy, and Air Force officers and some international officers as well. This experience allows the students the opportunity to learn from their peers in other services and even peers from within their own services who serve in different career fields. Students complete a service values survey at the beginning of the class to discern their preconceptions of officers from the other services. They rate their perceptions of officers from the four services on a scale of 1 to 7 among nine characteristics: Motivating, Enthusiastic, Empathetic, Competent, Respectful, Bold, Loyal, Selfless, and Principled. Figure 2 shows a typical graph of how the students rate their peers from the other services. Air Force officers rate high on empathy as perceived by students, while Marine officers typically rate the lowest on empathy. However, Marines usually rate the highest for motivating, enthusiasm, and boldness. Air Force officers rate high for competence, but typically lowest among the four services for boldness.

Figure 2: Pre-Acculturation Service Values Graph

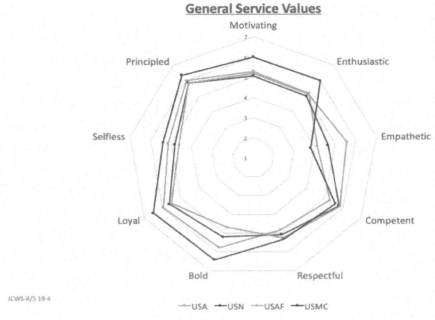

JCWS-H/S 19-4

Source: Joint Forces Staff College. "JCWS Service Values Survey"

An interesting trend invariably occurs over the ten-week course as officers work together and learn about the other services, their perceptions of officers from those other services changes. Figure 3 shows the pre- and post- Joint Acculturation Survey results. Perceptions of all the services improve, but notably, the impressions of Marines increase significantly on the Empathy characteristic. Officers perceive Air Force officers as more bold and selfless after the ten weeks. Army officers are perceived higher for competence and empathy. While this consistently occurs when officers share their experiences and work together in a concentrated academic environment, a similar effect likely occurs when officers from the different services work together and increase their familiarity in the working environment of a joint organization as well.

Figure 3: Post-Acculturation Survey Results Graph

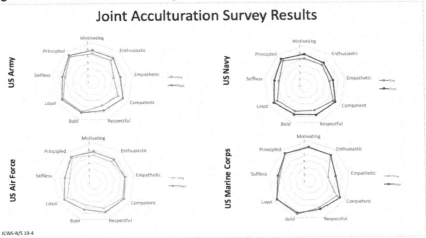

Source: Joint Forces Staff College. "JCWS Acculturation Survey Results"

United States Coast Guard

The United States Coast Guard stands as a highly unique military service. Unlike the other military branches, the Coast Guard falls under the Department of Homeland Security and answers to that Secretary. The Coast Guard organizes, trains, and equips its resources to be multi-mission capable. As a part of the Department of Homeland Security, it plays an active role in Homeland Security and Homeland Defense missions. The Coast Guard recognized August 4, 1790, as its birthday when Congress authorized then-Secretary of the Treasury, Alexander Hamilton, to build ten cutters to protect the new country's revenue.[30] Throughout its history, the Coast Guard remained part of the Department of the Treasury until the establishment of the Department of Homeland Security in 2002.

The U.S. Coast Guard has the following mission statement:

"The mission of the United States Coast Guard is to ensure our Nation's maritime safety, security and stewardship."[31]

Additionally, the Coast Guard manages six operational mission programs that oversee 11 missions defined in the Homeland Security Act of 2002. These 11 missions include:

1. Ports, Waterways, and Coastal Security
2. Drug Interdiction
3. Aids to Navigation
4. Search and Rescue
5. Living Marine Resources
6. Marine Safety
7. Defense Readiness (National Security and Military Preparedness
8. Migrant Interdiction
9. Maritime Environmental Protection
10. Polar, Ice, & Alaska Operations (including International Ice Patrol)
11. Law Enforcement

(Source: https://www.history.uscg.mil/home/Missions/)

Unlike the other military services that have virtually no law enforcement authority due to the *Posse Comitatus* Act, the Coast Guard possesses law enforcement authorities. However, the Coast Guard can operate under the Department of the Navy in times of war or when directed by the President.[32]

Officers assigned to one of the overseas Combatant Commands will likely have limited interaction with the U.S. Coast Guard. However, officers assigned to the Joint Staff, U.S. Northern Command, or U.S. Southern Command will probably have extensive interactions with Coast Guard personnel since these commands plan and conduct missions that may include Homeland Security and Homeland Defense considerations. Having an understanding of the Coast Guard's history, missions, and authorities will enable a joint officer to better coordinate with and leverage the unique capabilities and authorities the Coast Guard brings.

1   Department of the Army, *Organization,* Headquarters U.S. Army, 2019. https://www.army.mil/info/organization/

2   R.M. Swain and A. C. Pierce (Eds.) "Service Identity and Joint Warfighting," *The Armed Forces Officer,* (Washington DC: NDU Press, 2017), 131–132.

3   Swain and Pierce, "Service Identity," 132.

4   James M. Smith. "Service Cultures, Joint Cultures, and the US Military" *Airman-Scholar,* Winter 1998, 4.

5   Swain and Pierce, "Service Identity," 133.

6   Swain and Pierce, "Service Identity," 134.

7   Swain and Pierce, "Service Identity," 134.

8   Swain and Pierce, "Service Identity," 135.

9   U.S. Marine Corps, Who We Are, *Our Purpose,* https://www.marines.com/who-we-are/our-purpose.html

10 U.S. Marine Corps, *Our Legacy: Battles Through Time.* https://www.marines.com/who-we-are/our-legacy/battles-through-time.html

11 U.S. Marine Corps, *Our Legacy: Battles Through Time.*

12 U.S. Marine Corps, *Our Legacy: Battles Through Time.*

13 U.S. Marine Corps, *Our Legacy: Battles Through Time.*

14 U.S. Marine Corps, *Our Legacy: Battles Through Time.*

15 U.S. Marine Corps, *Our Legacy: Battles Through Time.*

16 U.S. Marine Corps, *Our Purpose*

17 Logan Nye, "11 Legends of the Marine Corps," *We Are the Mighty,* https://www.wearethemighty.com/articles/10-legendary-heroes-us-marine-corps

18 Smith, "Service Cultures," 5.

19 Smith, "Service Cultures," 5.

20 Department of the Navy, Secretary of the Navy Year 3 Strategic Vision, Goals, and Implementation Guidance, Fiscal Years 2020–2023. https://www.navy.mil/strategic/Department_of_the_Navy_Strategic_Guidance_FY2020.pdf

21 Smith, "Service Cultures,"

22 Interview with CDR Daniel Orchard-Hayes, USN, February 6, 2020.

23 Department of the Air Force, *Biographies,* https://www.af.mil/About-Us/Biographies/Display/Article/107811/general-henry-h-arnold

24 Department of the Air Force, *Air Force Mission,* www.airforce.com/mission

25 Smith, "Service Cultures," 6.

26 U.S. Air Force Space Command, *History,* https://www.afspc.af.mil/About-Us/AFSPC-History/

27 U.S. Air Force Space Command, *History.*

28 U.S. Space Command, *Fact Sheet*, https://www.spacecom.mil/About/Fact-Sheets-Editor/Article/1948216/united-states-space-command-fact-sheet/

29 United States Space Force, *What's the Space Force*, https://www.spaceforce.mil/About-Us/FAQs/Whats-the-Space-Force

30 U.S. Coast Guard, *Timeline*, https://www.history.uscg.mil/Complete-Time-Line/Time-Line-1700-1800

31 U.S. Coast Guard, *Missions*, https://www.history.uscg.mil/home.Missions

32 Joint Forces Staff College. Student Text 1, The Joint Staff Officer's Guide. (8th Ed.). National Defense University, 2019, 7–14.

CHAPTER 3:
Overview of Joint Leadership

"During my eighty-seven years, I have witnessed a whole succession of technological revolutions. But none of them has done away with the need for character in the individual or the ability to think."

— *Bernard Mannes Baruch*

Up to this point in their careers, officers will have developed strong familiarization in their respective service, and built tremendous credibility through proficiency in their primary career field. An Air Force aviator will have strong credibility in airpower, an Army Infantry officer will know how to lead soldiers in a ground combat situation, and a Naval officer will have a clear understanding of how to lead a department on a ship or even command a ship and its crew of sailors on the open seas. However, once these diverse personnel with their unique expertise and organizational cultures come together, leading them in a joint environment means new opportunities and challenges. It will help to review some leadership basics and discuss the similarities and differences between how those principles apply in a joint and combined organization versus a small tactical-level organization comprised exclusively of people from the same service. While there is no single universally agreed-upon definition for leadership, Peter Northouse defines leadership as "a process whereby an individual influences a group of individuals to achieve a common goal"[1] This simple definition identifies the two functions a joint leader must seek to achieve: Setting a clear, common goal, and influencing the individuals in their organization to work together to achieve that goal.

Officers who have led their respective service personnel in tactical-level units will find that some leadership practices are universal, but that the level of personnel they will lead in a joint organization will require adjustments for a different situation. Hersey and Blanchard proposed the Situational Approach (Figure 4) to leadership based on how leaders can lead and adapt their leadership style to different situations.[2] Drill instructors leading new basic trainees newly entering the military will apply a very directive (S1) approach. Recruits have minimal experience and are just beginning their indoctrination into the military's way of doing things. They focus on learning basics like how to wear the uniform properly, how to follow orders, and how to pay attention to details. As these new personnel graduate from basic training and attend technical schools to learn their jobs, they gradually transition from an S1 style and to more of a Coaching style. New officers similarly go through their respective training programs to learn how to fly an aircraft, drive a ship, lead a small infantry unit, or operate a satellite as part of a space operations crew. Officers leading these individuals will find that these followers have some competence and varying commitment to the mission, so they can use a mix of Coaching and Supporting leadership style. As followers progress in their experience and commitment to the organization, leaders can go to a full Supporting leadership (D3) style.

Figure 4: Hersey & Blanchard Situational Leadership Model

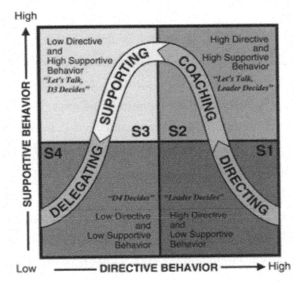

Source: Willie Vigil, "Applying the Situational Leadership Approach" Penn State University

Rarely can leaders in tactical-level units go entirely to a Delegating leadership style. Once officers reach the small unit commander level, they will have majors, captains, and senior enlisted personnel working for them that have ten or more years of experience and high commitment to the organizational mission. However, many officers going to a joint staff assignment have not gained battalion, squadron, or ship command experience.

A leader in a joint organization will lead a branch filled primarily with mid-level officers (Majors and Lieutenant Colonels) who have 10–15 years of experience. These officers have become experts in their respective service and career fields. They typically have a very high commitment to the mission. The fact that their services selected them to go to a joint assignment usually means they have proven themselves as highly capable and competent officers. Leading these officers using a Directing (S1) or Coaching (S2) leadership style will not work for long. A joint leader will want to begin with a Supporting (S3) leadership style initially, particularly for newly arriving officers as they learn about their job and role in the joint organization and grow accustomed to the organizational rules and culture. A leader applying the Supporting style will use more "listening, praising, ask for input, and give feedback."[3] As these officers grow into their role in the first few months, the joint leader can seek to achieve the Delegating (S4) leadership style. This delegation allows followers to have more involvement in planning, a stronger say in deciding the details, and inputs into setting the organizational goals. This style will both ease the leader's burden while also mentor and develop those officers to prepare them to lead in the joint and combined organization in the future.

Officers will find that most joint and combined organizations have grown exceedingly reliant on technology and information technology systems to perform their work. While helpful for coordination, technologies like email, PowerPoint, and Task Management Tools (TMTs) have begun to replace real face-to-face communications and have exerted detrimental effects on leadership. All the technologies may ease coordination and help with knowledge management, but they don't replace the need for leadership and leadership vision. As Bernard Baruch stated, technology has never successfully replaced the need for character and the ability to think in leaders. Joint leaders should seek to avoid growing too reliant on technologies and focus on long-standing and well-proven leadership principles to lead officers from other services and nations.

Northouse discussed the central role culture can play in leadership. As mentioned in the previous chapter, officers bring many cultures with them to their joint assignments. They bring their respective service cultures and subcultures from their career fields. International officers will also bring cultures from their countries as well. Officers assigned to U.S. Forces in Japan will find them frequently working with and potentially leading Japanese Self Defense Force (JSDF) personnel. Officers assigned to U.S. Forces Korea will interact with Republic of Korea officers. Leaders working in European Command or NATO will interact with European partner nations' personnel. While it's important to understand some of the cultural norms that will make or break a joint leader working in these environments, certain leader attributes work universally across all global cultures.

Northouse stated that the spread of globalization since World War II has created the need for leaders to develop their competence in cross-cultural awareness. Particularly helpful for joint leaders will be understanding *The GLOBE Study of 62 Societies.*[4] While very detailed in identifying ten cultural dimensions and breaking the countries analyzed up into ten regional country clusters, the key takeaway from this study for a joint leader is to understand the Universally Desirable Leadership Attributes (Figure 5) and the Universally Undesirable Leadership Attributes (Figure 6). Leaders in a joint organization, who have experience leading in

Figure 5: Universally Desired Leadership Attributes

Trustworthy	Just	Honest
Has foresight	Plans ahead	Encouraging
Positive	Dynamic	Motive arouser
Confidence builder	Decisive	Effective bargainer
Intelligent	Motivational	Dependable
Win-Win problem solver	Communicative	Informed
Administratively skilled	Coordinative	Team builder
Excellence orientated		

Source: Peter G. Northouse, "Leadership: Theory and Practice, 6th Ed.

their respective Services will recognize that many of these attributes align with their Service's core values and have a track record of success in any leader situation. Trustworthiness, honesty, planning ahead, intelligence, and motivational behaviors will work for any followers. Regardless of service, nationality, or agency, followers will view a leader who exhibits these attributes favorably and want to work for them. On the other hand, the GLOBE Study also identified universally undesirable leader attributes (Figure 6). Leaders who don't work well with others, exhibit authoritarian tendencies, or don't communicate clearly will turn followers off.

Figure 6: Universally Undesirable Leadership Attributes

Loner	Asocial	Noncooperative
Irritable	Nonexplicit	Egocentric
Ruthless	Dictatorial	

Source: Peter G. Northouse, "Leadership: Theory and Practice, 6th Ed.

Historical Examples

Dwight Eisenhower captured the essence of these leadership traits in his *Crusade in Europe* memoir. As the Supreme Allied Commander in Europe (SACEUR), Eisenhower had to build a coalition comprised of dominant personalities while balancing the equities of multiple services and nations. Eisenhower had to work for President Roosevelt and Prime Minister Winston Churchill, both strong national leaders on the global stage. He had to work with British Field Marshall Montgomery, French leader Charles De Gaulle, and American generals George Patton and Omar Bradley. Eisenhower deftly managed these senior leaders and dominating personalities to build the coalition, hold it together for three years, and achieve the goal of victory in Europe. He had to "alternatively charm, bully, agree, hire, or fire with lightning speed; and his instincts about people were nearly always right."[5]

By contrast, General Douglas MacArthur also led a multi-service, binational coalition in the Pacific theater during World War II. From 1942–1945, MacArthur led the Southwest Pacific Area which included a coalition of US and Australian military forces at the operational level.[6] MacArthur came from the US Army and had a strong foothold in the Army culture. However, he relied heavily on the Navy, Army Air Corps, and the Marine Corps to enable his operations against Japan. At the beginning of the coalition, when MacArthur escaped from the Philippines to Australia and made his infamous "I Shall Return" speech, MacArthur had virtually no U.S. military forces available. He relied most heavily on the Australians to provide forces to fulfill his plans. As the war progressed, and the U.S. began to provide more of the forces required, MacArthur's mercurial personality took over and dominated the coalition. By the last year of the war, the US dominated the alliance, and MacArthur largely pushed the Australian leaders aside. Peter Dean asserts that the basis for a sound coalition military effort includes common doctrine, continuous exchanges of military personnel, interoperability, and combined training and exercises.[7] Most of these did not exist in the Southwest Pacific Ocean Area in 1942.[8] General MacArthur's strong personality and ambitions proved the dominating factor in the coalition, and his "refusal to set up a truly joint and combined headquarters" further complicated this relationship.[9]

Today, the United States, Australia, and New Zealand have a robust military-to-military relationship. In 2015, the countries held their biannual Joint Exercise KEEN EDGE, which included a Combined Task Force staff with Australian, New Zealand, and US officers working together on a combined staff. While commanded by a US Navy Vice Admiral, the Deputy Commanding General for the Task Force was an Australian Army general. Australian officers also filled other key positions throughout the staff organization, making it truly a combined organization. The U.S. also does regular combined exercises with Japan, Korea, NATO, and other countries and organizations. These combined exercises and training foster the relationships and improve interoperability between the militaries of the member nations. A US officer serving as a joint or combined leader in these organizations will have to work with and grow these relationships with officers from other countries, other services, and other specialty branches within those services. Applying the Universally Desirable Leadership Attributes will help in achieving success in this environment.

Other Leadership Theories

Transformational Leadership Theory offers another means for a joint leader to succeed and lead their organizations. Most traditional leadership models deal with a transactional leadership approach, which focuses on exchanges that occur between leaders and followers.[10] A leader needs the follower to accomplish a particular task. The leader offers a good performance appraisal in return for the follower accomplishing the task successfully. Teachers offering good grades or bosses offering bonuses and promotions in return for positive behavior practice transactional leadership.[11] By contrast, transformational leaders "engages with others and crates a connection that raises the level of motivation and morality in both the leader and follower."[12] A transactional leader focuses above just the tasks performed by the followers and seeks to improve follower performance and develop them to advance their potential. Northouse offered the four "I's" of Transformational Leadership: Idealized influence, Inspirational motivation, Intellectual stimulation, and Individualized consideration. Leaders seeking to develop idealized influence will act as strong role models for followers with the aspiration that followers will identify with them and want to emulate them. Leaders implementing inspirational motivation will communicate high expectations to followers and motivate them to commit to join and support a shared organizational vision. For a joint leader running a staff branch or directorate, they will provide a clear vision for this organization and inspire followers to commit to and support that vision. Leaders can achieve intellectual stimulation by encouraging followers to be creative and innovate. General George Patton once said, "Never tell your subordinates how to do things, tell them what to do and they will surprise you with their ingenuity." Similarly, a joint leader provides the vision and defines the goals, but provides followers latitude in how they accomplish the mission and achieve those goals. Finally, individualized consideration describes how leaders will seek to become good listeners. They talk to their followers face-to-face to learn their individual needs and wants and offer to support them. Giving a follower a high-profile project or the opportunity to brief a senior leader on an initiative or project the organization has worked on serves many purposes. It fosters commitment in the follower to have a sense of ownership in and participate in the development of the project and the briefing to communicate it. It also gives them experience in briefing and communicating with senior leaders. Finally, it builds the bench of the organization, so more personnel are available to brief in the future. All of these results will prove positive for the organization, the leader, and the followers.

Servant leadership also offers a lot for joint leaders seeking to lead personnel from multiple services and nations. Originated by Robert Greenleaf in the early 1970s, Servant Leadership theory has emerged as a prevailing theory that emphasizes leaders' role as attentiveness to follower needs, empowering others, and seeking to develop them to improve their capacities.[13] Servant leadership also works particularly well for military officers in a defense organization focused on service to the nation and service to others. Reviewing the Service's core values will clearly illustrate a parallel with Servant Leadership. The Army lists its seven core values as loyalty, duty, respect, selfless service, honor, integrity, and personal courage.[14] The Air Force espouses "Integrity first, Service before self, Excellence in all we do." The Navy and Marine Corps claim honor, courage, and commitment that form the basis of character. Robert Greenleaf defined servant leadership as follows:

> *"Servant leadership begins with the natural feeling that one wants to serve, to serve first. Then conscious choice brings one to aspire to lead… The difference manifests itself in the care taken by the servant—first to make sure that other people's highest priority needs are being served. The best test…is: do those served grow as persons; do they, while being served, become healthier, wiser, freer, more autonomous, more likely themselves to become servants?"*[15]

This definition characterizes key leader attributes a joint leader can apply to lead personnel from other services and other nations successfully. Effectively, the Services have loaned those officers to the joint organization. These officers are effectively out of their Service branch and their career field for the duration of their joint tour, so it is incumbent on their leaders to take care of them, help them grow, and give them opportunities to develop and prepare for that day when they will return to their home Service. Many of these officers will compete for command opportunities, and some will grow into the next generation of senior leaders. A few may ultimately return to the joint force as general or flag officers. However, this cannot occur if they stagnate or suffer career damage during their time in the joint organization. A joint leader seeking to apply servant leadership must apply some key characteristics of a servant leader: listening, empathy, foresight, stewardship, and commitment to the growth of their people.

1   Peter G. Northouse, *Leadership: Theory and Practice*, 6th Ed. (Washington DC: SAGE Publications, 2013), 5.

2   Northouse *Leadership*, 100.

3   Northouse, *Leadership*, 95.

4   Northouse, *Leadership*, 431.

5   Stavridis, *The Leader's Bookshelf*, 69.

6   Peter J. Dean, *MacArthur's Coalition: US and Australian Operations in the Southwest Pacific Ocean Area, 1942-1945* (Lawrence, KS: University Press of Kansas, 2018), 4.

7   Northouse, *Leadership*, 367.

8   Northouse, *Leadership*, 367.

9   Northouse, *Leadership*, 367.

10 Northouse, *Leadership*, 162.

11 Northouse, *Leadership*, 162.

12 Northouse, *Leadership*, 162.

13 Northouse, *Leadership*, 219

14 Department of the Army, *The Army Values,* 2019. www.army.mil

15 Robert K. Greenleaf, "The Servant As Leader" in *Leadership: Theory and Practice,* 6th Ed. Peter G. Northouse, 220.

CHAPTER 4:
Leadership Communication in a Joint and Combined Environment

"Leadership is solving problems. The day soldiers stop bringing you their problems is the day you have stopped leading them. They have either lost confidence that you can help or concluded you do not care. Either case is a failure of leadership."

— *General Colin Powell*

"Secure the Building!" There's a long-standing interservice joke about the different meanings of that phrase for officers of the military services. Tell an Army officer to "Secure the building," and they will call in a heavy artillery strike or an air strike to level the building to rubble. Tell a Marine to "secure the building," and he'll assemble a platoon of Marines with weapons and body armor. They'll storm the building, check every room to neutralize any hostile actors, and once every room has been cleared, declare the building "secured." Tell a naval officer to "Secure the building," and they'll lock up the rooms, sign off the end-of-day checklists, turn out the lights, lock the external doors, and go home for the day. An Air Force officer told to "secure the building" will get you a five-year lease on the building with an option to buy it.

While this joke plays upon some of the service cultures, stereotypes, and pokes some fun through interservice rivalries, it also captures some of the potential issues an officer assigned to a joint or combined organization may face when communicating with others. An officer assigned to a joint staff should invest time in learning and properly applying the joint terminology to reduce the chances of confusion or misunderstanding. The Department of Defense (DoD) has published a DoD Dictionary of Military and Associated Terms with the express purpose to supplement "standard English-language dictionaries and standardizes military and associated terminology to improve communication and mutual understanding within DOD with other US Government departments and agencies and among United States and its allies."[1] One classic example where officers can misuse words involves the terms "special forces" and "special operations." Military personnel and civilians often use these terms interchangeably, but they actually have significantly different meanings in a joint environment. The DoD Dictionary defines "special forces" as "United States Army forces organized, trained, and equipped to conduct special operations with an emphasis on unconventional warfare capabilities."[2] While well understood to refer solely to Army units and personnel, officers not tuned in to the special operations community will occasionally use the term "special forces" to wrongly refer to other service organizations such as the Navy SEALs or Air Force Pararescue operators. The DoD Dictionary defines "special operations" as "operations requiring unique modes of employment, tactical techniques, equipment and training often conducted in hostile, denied, or politically sensitive environments and characterized by one or more of the following: time sensitive, clandestine, low visibility, conducted with and/or through indigenous forces, requiring regional expertise, and/or a high degree of risk."[3] All the services have special operations forces, units and personnel specially organized, trained, and equipped to conduct joint operations, but only the Army has "special forces" who conduct special operations. The key takeaway for an officer assigned to a joint organization is to realize the importance of understanding and using the correct terminology while communicating in a joint organization.

Another key aspect to leadership communications in any organization is to understand the components of communication. Communication scholar

David Barnlund identified five principles reflecting the core components of human communication.[4]

1. Communication is a **process**, dynamic and ever-changing
2. Communication is **circular**, not linear
3. Communication is **complex**
4. Communication is **irreversible**
5. Communication involves **total personality**

These components particularly manifest when officers from different services communicate in a joint or combined environment. For a leader in a joint organization, communications involve more than just sharing relevant information for a given task and planning effort. These communications also include learning between the participants about the other services. The circular nature of communication means that the communication involves a continuous feedback loop between the participants. "Effective communicators pay close attention to the messages being sent to them as they talk to others."[5]

Communications prove complex in any organization. Barnlund explained that in any conversation between two people, there are really six people involved in the conversation.[6]

1. Who you think you are
2. Who you think the other person is
3. Who you think the other person thinks you are
4. Who the other person thinks he or she is
5. Who the other person thinks you are
6. Who the other person thinks you think he or she is[7]

This complexity increases in a joint and combined environment blending officers from multiple services and multiple nations. When an Air Force officer communicates with an Army or Navy officer, they will likely apply preconceived notions, either consciously or subconsciously, of what they think about officers of those services. They will also have cognizance of what those other services may think about them. This complexity opens the possibility of miscommunication or faulty perceptions.

Communication is also irreversible. This is true of verbal communications, but even more true when communicating via written correspondence like email. A leader communicating to followers exerts greater influence with their communications than peers, and what a leader chooses to say and how they say it implies priorities. However, once a leader communicates a message, there is no way to "un-communicate" what was said, particularly if it was uttered during a heated conversation influenced by emotions.[8] Finally, communication "involves the total personality" that cannot be separated from the person saying it.[9]

Since communication contains many components and complexities, the most effective leadership communications happen during face-to-face conversations. While a lot of correspondence and coordination at a joint headquarters happens via emails and task management tools due to their ease of use, leaders need to see their people and their followers need to see them. This can occur through regular, purposeful staff meetings to review organizational tasks and priorities as well as through one-on-one meetings to conduct more personal conversations and feedback sessions. Many senior leaders succumb to the common pitfall of allowing these face-to-face communication opportunities to diminish and replace them almost exclusively with impersonal email messages. While an email may convey the basic information and offers a way to mass message a large number of recipients quickly, it dispenses with the major part of communication, the nonverbal component. Joint leaders can use the Communication Dos and Don'ts list to help keep themselves on track and try to maintain a positive work climate with healthy two-way communications.

Communication Dos

1.   **Do**: Get to know your peers and followers personally
2.   **Do**: Use face-to-face communications when possible to establish relationships
3.   **Do**: Engage in constructive leadership behavior

4. **Do**: Talk about "We" and "Us" rather than "I" and "Me"

5. **Do**: Follow through. Followers will respect those who keep their word and consistently do what they say

6. **Do**: Remember that communications are two-way

7. **Do**: Become an expert. Constantly seek to learn and build your expertise and credibility

8. **Do**: Model the behavior you want followers to emulate

9. **Do**: Communicate professionally and with respect

10. **Do**: Set standards, communicate those clearly, and hold organization members accountable

Communication Don'ts

1. **Don't**: Lead from afar. Visit your people in their workspaces

2. **Don't**: Use e-mail or other electronic communications as a substitute for face-to-face communications

3. **Don't**: Engage in tyrannical leadership behavior

4. **Don't**: Allow a disconnect to form between leader behavior and leader communications

Briefings

Joint headquarters organizations commonly use briefings as a means to communicate to personnel as well as senior leaders. Briefings typically come with one of two purposes. Informational briefings seek to deliver information and background on a given topic. These can seek to provide a bottom-line impact of a situation, offer a detailed description of the operational environment (OE), and the linkages and potential impacts. Common briefings officers will see on a regular basis include Operations and Intelligence briefings that provide a snapshot of current operations and the relevant intelligence to provide background and forecasts of what may occur in the near-term. The second type of briefing is a Decision Briefing. This briefing will offer an overview of the operational environment and relevant actors, present detailed analysis that joint planners will use to discern what to do about an ongoing or emerging situation, develop and present alternatives for the decision-maker, and offer a recommendation. Ultimately the commander will have to digest the information and recommendations and make a decision on what course of action to pursue.

Each command and joint organization will have a slide template that officers should use when preparing briefings. Rarely will an officer have to reinvent the wheel and develop a slide presentation from scratch. The general format across all military organizations will include a title slide with appropriate classification markings and the briefer's name and office, an overview slide with an outline of the contents, the content slides, and a repeat of the overview slide. Generally, the higher the rank of the officer receiving the briefing, the lower the number of slides in the briefing. As a general rule of thumb, a slide presentation for a one-hour briefing to staff officers will consist of around 20–25 slides maximum. As the presentation goes higher to the Combatant Commander level, the presentation should condense such that the Commander would receive the information in about 8–10 slides maximum. The Combatant Commander often receives multiple briefings each day, and processes overwhelming amounts of information from the staff in the organization and senior leaders outside the organization. While the staff officers working and coordinating on an issue will need to understand the finite details of the issue, as the presentation moves up the chain to the Director and finally the Commander level, these briefings need to provide a high-level overview with only those key pieces of information needed for the commander to know and ultimately make a decision.

During Joint Planning efforts, the planning team will typically have particular touchpoints with key leaders and often the commander as they step through the Joint Planning Process (JPP). The joint planning doctrine (JP 5-0) outlines that the planning group will conduct three briefings to the commander, and offers templates for a recommended structure and key items for these briefings. The first will be the Mission Analysis briefing to get the commander's approval on key aspects of the plan. Second, the planning team will present the Course of Action (COA) briefing to show the commander the two or three different possible options the planning team developed and get the commander's initial guidance on evaluation criteria to analyze the courses of action. Finally, the planning team will conduct analysis and wargaming, compare the courses, and present a third briefing to the commander to recommend a course of action. These three briefings contain significant amounts of information and may be the exception to the rule to keep briefings to the commander smaller than ten slides.

Emails

The most common form of communication and coordination in a joint organization, aside from face-to-face verbal communication, involves email. Officers routinely coordinate work and schedule meetings using email as a quick means to exchange information, send a product to colleagues for them to review and provide input, or to provide information to senior officers. Each joint organization likely has rules and best practices regarding email messages. Two ways an officer can find themselves in trouble quickly with email is to send classified information over an unclassified system and to type a response in anger and hit the "Send" button too soon.

U.S. Central Command used the "BLIND" format and required all staff personnel to use this format for emails. The BLIND format uses the following structure

B/L: (This is the bottom-line purpose of the email message in two or three concise sentences

I: Information, often in bullet format that is key for the recipient to know regarding the issue

N: Next action: This section offers the next action that needs to occur. Does the recipient need to make a decision, provide coordination on the topic, approve an action, or simply gain situational awareness about the subject?

D: Details. This section will have the detailed information. While the reader should have the essential information required in the top three sections, this will offer a thorough background, steps taken, and relevance for the reader.

This format worked for U.S. Central Command in 2010 but likely changed over time as new commanders took over and required changes for how they like to receive and assimilate information. The key takeaway for a joint officer is to seek to limit emails to those required to accomplish the tasks, write messages in a concise manner that makes it easy for the reader to understand and take the appropriate actions, and follow the applicable business rules in the joint organizations where they work.

Senior executive-level leaders can receive 200 to 300 emails a day on widely varying topics. The key for joint staff officers when preparing an email message, particularly to senior officers, is to write clear and concise messages that quickly convey the most important high-level information. Put yourself in the role of that senior leader and try to anticipate what they need as the reader of that email. What are the key takeaways they need to grasp in a short period of time that are relevant and will help them synthesize that information and take the appropriate decisions when required?

1   Office of the Chairman of the Joint Chiefs of Staff, *DOD Dictionary of Military and Associated Terms*, (Washington DC: The Joint Staff, November 2019), i.

2   Office of the Chairman, *DOD Dictionary of Military and Associated Terms*, (199.

3   Office of the Chairman, *DOD Dictionary of Military and Associated Terms*, 199–200.

4   Michael Z. Hackman and Craig E. Johnson, *Leadership: A Communication Perspective*, 6th Ed. (Long Grove, IL: Waveland Press, Inc., 2013), 6.

5   Hackman and Johnson, *Leadership: A Communication Perspective*, 9.

6   Hackman and Johnson, *Leadership: A Communication Perspective*, 9.

7   Hackman and Johnson, *Leadership: A Communication Perspective*, 9.

8   Hackman and Johnson, *Leadership: A Communication Perspective*, 10.

9   Hackman and Johnson, *Leadership: A Communication Perspective*, 10.

CHAPTER 5:
Developing Strategy for Joint Organizations

Strategy without tactics is the slowest route to victory. Tactics without strategy is the noise before defeat.

— *Sun Tzu*

Developing and implementing strategy for a small organization can present significant challenges. Developing and implementing strategy for a Defense Department that consists of nearly three million military and civilian personnel, operating around the world and with an annual budget exceeding $750 billion is many orders of magnitude harder. The DoD implements its departmental strategy as part of the larger U.S. government, which requires coordination between other U.S. government agencies (interagency), other intergovernmental organizations such as the United Nations (UN), Economic Community of West African States (ECOWAS), the Association of Southeast Asian Nations (ASEAN), and other nations' militaries (multinational), the JIIM environment. When discussing national strategy, strategists often describe U.S. policy implementation in terms of the four instruments of national power. These four include Diplomacy, Information, Military, and Economic instruments, commonly referred to as the DIME. The DoD focuses its attention on the Military (M in DIME), but the other three instruments heavily influence Defense strategy and vice versa. Joint planners will often find themselves coordinating their efforts with the State Department and U.S. Embassy personnel in their region to ensure consideration of the Diplomatic, Informational, and Economic instruments as they develop and implement strategy that supports the U.S. interests.

U.S. national and defense strategy has evolved very hierarchically. Grand Strategy resides at the highest level. Grand strategies often transcend presidential administrations and can last for decades or even centuries. The Monroe Doctrine, enacted by President Monroe in the early 1800s, endured through the twentieth century and beyond. Following World War I, the United States followed a very isolationist strategy, seeking to disentangle itself from the European powers. Despite this isolationist stance that lasted for 20 years, the United States found itself drawn into Europe's problems again and had to fight in World War II. The United States allied itself with Great Britain and the Soviet Union to form the Allies fighting against the Axis powers of Germany, Japan, and Italy. While victory in World War II left the Allies with an emotional high, this alliance soon disintegrated as the United States and the Soviet Union became rivals in the post-World War world. As the Soviet Union attempted to spread its influence and proliferate Communism around the world, President Truman implemented the Grand Strategy of "Containment," which guided the United States policy for more than four decades. This grand strategy drove the United States to build up its military again in the ensuing years, fight wars in Korea and Vietnam, build a massive nuclear triad comprised of bombers, intercontinental ballistic missiles, and nuclear submarines, and culminated in the late 1960s with the Space Race.

Below Grand Strategy, joint officers will find themselves discussing and planning at three levels of warfare: Tactical, Operational, and Strategic. Officers primarily serve at the tactical level early in their careers when they learn how to operate their ship or aircraft or lead their small ground units. By the time officers reach the milestone of a joint assignment, they have become experts at the tactical level of warfare for their respective platforms. Army majors know how to command their infantry or tank companies and achieve success on the ground. Navy officers know how to drive their ship or fly their aircraft. Air Force officers know how to fly their aircraft or operate their space systems, and Marines know their tactical-level jobs with high proficiency. With 10–15 years of experience, these officers have become experts in their respective service and ready to lead mid-sized units of 100-500 personnel organized into Army or Marine battalions, squadrons, or to command ships with crews of a few hundred sailors.

The Strategic level describes activities that primarily occur inside the Washington DC Beltway. The President issues a National Security Strategy (NSS) on a biennial basis, which outlines the high-level strategic goals for the nation. The NSS includes considerations for all four instruments of national power: Diplomatic, Informational, Military, and Economic (DIME), and sets the direction for all U.S. government departments. The State Department concentrates on the Diplomatic instrument. The State Department, along with the Treasury Department and Commerce Department, work on international trade and guiding economic strategy. All departments work in the Informational part, but the Department of Defense has almost exclusive claim to the Military instrument. The Secretary of Defense publishes a National Defense Strategy (NDS) which concentrates and expands almost exclusively on the military aspects of the national strategy. Finally, the Chairman of the Joint Chiefs of Staff (CJCS) publishes a National Military Strategy, which provides guidance for the services and the Combatant Commands. According to Derek Reveron and James Cook, the Department of Defense "increasingly requires strategy to operate in a fiscally constrained environment."[1]

Donald Neuchterlein proposed that all nations have interests, and that these interests run along a "four-tiered scale of priorities," which determine how much value a nation "attaches to specific foreign policy issues."[2] Neuchterlein defined these four priority levels as follows:

1. Survival interests – existential threats that place the nation's survival in peril

2. Vital interests – threats that require the nation to take strong measures within a short period of time, including military action if necessary, to prevent probable serious harm to the nation's security

3.   Major interests – the nation could face serious harm if it takes no action to counter an unfavorable trend abroad

4.   Peripheral (minor) interests – little if any harm will occur to the nation if the President adopts a "wait and see" policy[3]

Planners should apply this lens to assess where issues in their region of the world will likely fall in terms of U.S. interests and priorities. This determination will guide planners in determining how much resources they can count on for a given planning effort, and how much resources national policymakers will commit to the effort. Reveron and Cook offered a simple description, defining vital interests as those "we are willing to die for," important interests as those "we are willing to fight for," and peripheral interests as those "we are willing to pay for." The following excerpt from Dwight Eisenhower's book, *Crusade in Europe*, captures how the United States and Congress quickly transitioned from perceiving the threat overseas from Germany and Japan traversing this scale from a peripheral interest in 1940 to a survival interest following the Pearl Harbor attack in December 1941.

> "The American people still believed that the distance provided adequate insulation between us and any conflict in Europe or Asia. Comparatively few understood the direct relationship between American prosperity and physical safety on the one hand, and on the other the existence of a free world beyond our shores. Consequently, the only Americans who thought about preparation for war were a few professionals in the armed services and those far-seeing statesmen who understood that American isolation from any major conflict was now completely improbably

In the spring of 1940, with the German seizure of Denmark and Norway, the blitz that swept from the Rhine through France to the Bay of Biscay, and the crippled retreat of the British Army from Dunkirk, America began to grow uneasy. By the middle of June, the Regular Army's authorized strength had been increased to 375,000. By the end of August, Congress has authorized the mobilization of the National Guard; six weeks later Selective Service was in operation. By the summer of 1941 the Army of the United States, composed of regulars, Guardsmen, and citizen soldiers, numbered 1,500,000. No larger peacetime force had ever been mustered by this country. It was, nevertheless, only a temporary compromise with international fact.

The million men who had come into the Army through the National Guard and Selective Service could not be required to serve anywhere outside the Western Hemisphere or for more than twelve months at home. In the summer of 1941, consequently, with the Germans racing across Russia and their Japanese ally unmistakably preparing for the conquest of the far Pacific, the Army could only feebly reinforce overseas garrisons.

The attack on Pearl Harbor was less than four months away when, by a one-vote margin in the House of Representatives, the Congress passed the Selective Service Extension Act, permitting the movement of all Army components overseas and extending the term of service. The congressional action can be attributed largely to the personal intervention of General George C. Marshall, who had already attained a public stature that gave weight to his urgent warning. But even he could not entirely overcome the conviction that an all-out effort for defense was unnecessary. Limitations on service, such as the release of men of the age of twenty-eight, reflected a continuing belief that there was no immediate danger.

> This for two years, as war engulfed the world outside the Americas and the Axis drove relentlessly toward military domination of the globe, each increase in size, efficiency, and appropriations of the armed services was the result of a corresponding decrease in the complacency of the American people. But their hesitation to abandon compromise for decisive action could not be wholly dispelled until Pearl Harbor converted the issue into a struggle for survival."
>
> *Source:* Dwight D. Eisenhower, "Crusade in Europe" 1948

Ultimately, all strategy guides priorities as national and senior military leaders seek to balance the ends, way, and means available to accomplish our national objectives, and manage the risk associated with any imbalance. Art Lykke visualized this Ends/Ways/Means imbalance as a three-legged stool, with the three legs representing Ends, Ways, and Means, respectively. The term "**Ends**" describes "what" we seek to accomplish.[4] **Ways** describe "how" we will employ resources to achieve the ends, and **Means** explains what specific resources are available to employ to achieve the ends. In a perfect world, Ends are finite, Means are infinite, and there are minimal limits to the ways we can employ those means. In reality, our desired ends are vast, and national resources are limited. As a result, our national strategy must seek the best way to employ those limited resources and define priorities for ends we will seek to achieve first.

Figure 7: Levels of War and Hierarchy of Strategy

Levels of War and Hierarchy of Strategy

Source: Harry R. Yarger, "Strategic Theory for the 21st Century"

The perpetual imbalance between these three legs highlights where strategic risk resides, and it falls on senior leaders to mitigate this risk, balance the three legs, and determine what priorities to set and where they can and cannot accept risk.

The Operational level resides at the nexus between the Strategic and Tactical levels (Figure 7). Joint commands reside in this nexus, and almost all of the planning and staff work officers working in a joint organization will occur at this level and seek to translate strategic-level guidance and direction into usable policies and plans that direct tactical forces on what they need to do in the event of a future contingency. Combatant Commanders will first seek to develop theater strategies for their respective Areas of Responsibility. These theater strategies, nested within the larger national strategy, will include a detailed description of the operational environment that includes allies, potential adversaries, geographic conditions, and other relevant actors. Indo-Pacific Command, for example, would describe the entire Pacific Rim and the countries present including, Japan, Korea, China, Taiwan, Indonesia, the Philippines, Australia, and others. Since much of the Indo-Pacific Command's area of responsibility consists of the Pacific Ocean, naval power and air power will play a significant role in any theater strategy. Sea lanes, ocean conditions, typhoon season, and tsunamis – all present challenges to any theater strategy. Once the commander and staff clearly define the operational environment, they will identify problems in that operational environment they seek to solve and the desired conditions they will work towards in the coming years to shape that environment and improve it for the United States' and its allies' interests. Once the commander identifies those desired ends, the next step involves identifying the approach to take to achieve those desired conditions. This approach begins to identify the ends, describe the means (i.e., resources available), and determine the ways to achieve those ends.

One of the most difficult challenges joint officers face involves raising their thought processes from their core tactical expertise and thinking at the operational level. An Army officer will be an expert in ground combat tactics and know how to lead a small unit to achieve particular tasks. An Air Force pilot will be the expert in tactics, techniques, and procedures to fly their airframe and defeat an adversary. The same goes for Navy and Marine officers in their respective combat specialties. All of these experts will clearly understand how to employ their respective service's forces. However, the operational level seeks to focus on "what" to accomplish rather than perfecting the "how." Operational-level planners attempt to answer the question, "Are we doing the right things?" rather than "Are we doing things right?"

The Joint Strategic Planning System

The Joint Strategic Planning System (JSPS) is "the method by which the Chairman fulfills his Title 10, U.S.C. responsibilities, maintains a global perspective, and provides military advice to the Secretary of Defense and the President."[5] The JSPS (Figure 8) seems like an incredibly complex and bureaucratic system to the uninitiated. The Chairman of the Joint Chiefs Instruction 3100.01D (CJCSI

3100.01D) is the primary document that defines and describes the JSPS. Most officers have only experienced the tail end of the JSPS at their tactical-level jobs when they have to deploy and operate as part of a joint force during an operation or an exercise. A lot of activity goes on at the strategic level to plan the operations and determine the personnel and resources needed to conduct those operations and exercises. The Chairman of the Joint Chiefs of Staff is the seniormost military officer in the Department of Defense, and serves as the principal military adviser to the President and the Secretary of Defense. Despite his seniority, however, the Chairman exercises no direct command authority over the U.S. military forces. By law, the Chairman performs six functions in his role.

1. Providing strategic direction for the Armed Forces
2. Conducting strategic and contingency planning
3. Assessing comprehensive joint readiness
4. Managing Joint Force Development
5. Fostering joint capability development
6. Advising on global military integration

These six roles make the Chairman the central figure in the Department of Defense's efforts to determine what size force we have, what weapons systems the services develop, where to focus resources, and how to gather and meet needs determined by the Combatant Commanders. At its core, the Joint Strategic Planning System provides a formal mechanism for the Chairman to define clearly the ends the commands will seek, determines the means (i.e., resources) that will be available for planning, and provides guidance on the ways Combatant Commanders will endeavor to meet the strategic guidance and help achieve the United States' national interests.

Figure 8: Joint Strategic Planning System (JSPS)

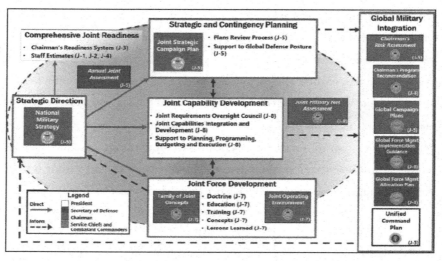

Source: CJCSI 3100.01D, "Joint Strategic Planning System"

First, the Chairman assists "the President and Secretary of Defense in providing for the strategic direction of the armed forces."[6] While the President's National Security Strategy presents broad, aspirational goals in terms of economics, diplomacy, trade, and security, the Chairman's National Military Strategy (NMS) focuses on the military instrument of national power. The President signs three guidance documents that provide direction: The National Security Strategy, the Unified Command Plan (UCP), and the Contingency Planning Guidance. The Secretary of Defense also provides strategic direction through three documents: The National Defense Strategy, the Defense Planning Guidance, and force employment guidance. Informed by this higher-level guidance, the Chairman prepares and submits the National Military Strategy as his "central strategy and planning document" that seeks to "translate policy guidance into Joint Force action," and provide "for the strategic direction of the armed forces."[7]

Second, the Chairman produces a five-year strategic plan that "operationalizes the National Military Strategy," called the Joint Strategic Campaign Plan (JSCP). The JSCP directs the Combatant Commanders to prepare plans and further offers guidance on what specific plans they require and what level of planning effort is required. The JSCP directs four types of campaign plans: Global Campaign Plans (GCPs), Regional Campaign Plans (RCPs), Functional Campaign Plans (FCPs), and Combatant Command Campaign Plans (CCPs). Joint officers assigned to a Combatant Command headquarters will primarily work with and develop CCPs that have replaced the previous Theater Campaign Plans.[8] Combatant Commands develop CCPs to analyze their respective theater operational environments, determine theater objectives, and develop broad approaches to achieve those objectives aligned with the Chairman's and higher strategic guidance and direction.

Third, U.S. law tasks the Chairman with evaluating the readiness of the joint force to fulfill its responsibilities and respond to major events. Day-to-day, the Chairman uses the Joint Force Readiness Review (JFRR), which combines and analyzes data pulled from the Defense Readiness Reporting System (DRRS). Officers from all services will likely be familiar with DRRS since tactical units across all the services report their readiness to perform their missions on a monthly basis using this system. The Chairman receives the consolidated and analyzed data from across the entire Department of Defense to make an assessment on the joint force's readiness to support Combatant Commands and execute the National Military Strategy. The Chairman conducts Integrated Campaign Plan (ICP) assessments to analyze and assess the Combatant Commands' abilities to successfully execute the highest priority contingency plans. The Chairman also submits a Joint Military Net Assessment (JMNA) annually to the Secretary of Defense. Finally, the Chairman conducts annual assessments on joint personnel through the Joint Personnel Estimate (JPE), the global environment through his Joint Strategic Intelligence Estimate (JSIE), and how well the joint force can project, support, and sustain itself through the Joint Logistics Estimate (JLE). All of these extensive assessments feed into building a comprehensive picture of Joint Readiness for the Chairman and Secretary of Defense.

Fourth, the Chairman must engage in activities to develop the Joint Force, including developing joint doctrine, formulating policies, standards, and actions for joint training, enacting policies for joint education, and formulating Joint

Force "concept development and experimentation" policies.[9] A key aspect for joint officers involves the joint professional military education (JPME) requirements. Following the Goldwater-Nichols Act and U.S. law, the Chairman has defined the requirements for JPME Level I, which officers typically get by attending any of their service Command & Staff Colleges. In order for an officer to earn the Joint Qualified Officer (JQO) designation, they must complete their joint assignment in a JDAL billet and complete JPME Level II (JPME II). Most officers receive their JPME II credit by attending the Joint and Combined Warfighting School (JCWS) 10-week residence course in Norfolk, VA. However, officers can also complete this education requirement by attending any of the senior service schools (i.e., Army, Navy, Air Force, Marine Corps, or National War College). In addition to this, the Chairman's Director, J-7, develops an annual list of up to six Special Areas of Emphasis (SAEs) that the Chairman approves, and the JPME institutions must then incorporate into their curriculum to educate the Joint Force.

Fifth, the Chairman conducts his role in Joint Capability Development by identifying new joint military capabilities, gathers the Combatant Command priorities and advises the Secretary of Defense on those priorities, and advises the Secretary of Defense on how "program recommendations and budget proposals" conform to priorities. Particularly in today's resource and budget-constrained environment, the Department of Defense must limit the funds and programs it requests from Congress. Programs and proposals that support multiple Combatant Command priorities will carry more weight than those that only support a single Command. The key mechanism for supporting the Chairman's Joint Capability Development function is through the Joint Requirements Oversight Council (JROC).[10] The Vice Chairman of the Joint Chiefs of Staff chairs the JROC as it assesses joint military capabilities, identifies and prioritizes capability gaps, and reviews and validates proposed capabilities to ensure they will adequately fill those gaps.[11] The JROC also develops recommendations for program costs and timelines for fielding new capabilities. This committee is the principal place where the Joint Force and the Services coordinate to ensure the capabilities and weapons systems that the Services seek to develop and acquire will actually support the future Joint Force and fill needs. Finally, the Chairman supports the Defense Secretary's Planning, Programming, Budgeting, and Execution (PPBE) process, which is the Secretary's "primary decision-making process for translating strategic guidance into resource allocation decisions."[12]

Sixth, the Chairman provides "advice to the President and the Secretary in matters relating to the global military strategic and operational integration."[13] In previous eras, Combatant Commands would develop plans for their respective regional Areas of Operation (AORs). However, with the increased emphasis on cross-domain warfare and the emergence of activities in the global space and cyber domains, Combatant Commands must increasingly account for events in other command regions. In 2016, the Secretary of Defense designated the Chairman as the global integrator, which requires the Chairman to "guide coordination across geographic, functional, and Service seams to ensure the Joint Force collectively expands its competitive advantages across a range of global challenges."[14] This means the Chairman must ensure all of the Combatant Commands recognize that their operations and activities have second and third-order effects that ripple outward and impact other Combatant Commands. Part of this function includes the requirement for a Global Campaign Plan and for the Chairman to recommend changes in resource allocation across the commands as required by changing world events.

Joint Force officers should be aware of the complex Joint Strategic Planning System, understand the six core functions it requires of the Chairman, and grasp the implications of this system and the Chairman's roles on their jobs as joint staff officers and joint planners. This entire system drives the personnel and system decisions of the services as they perform their organizing, training, and equipping roles, and ensures they make their decisions accounting for Joint Force needs.

Theater Strategies

Below the Grand Strategy and the National Strategic level, Combatant Commanders develop theater strategies for their respective Areas of Responsibility. These theater strategies, which typically examine a five-year time horizon, serve to provide the "combatant commander's vision for integrating and synchronizing military activities and operations with the other instruments of national power in order to achieve national strategic objectives."[15] This theater strategy links national strategic guidance to the operational level by providing the guidance for the development of a Theater Campaign Plan (TCP) that includes an operational approach to describe how the command will achieve the desired conditions in five years. Most of these activities involve "soft power" actions like security cooperation, engagement, assistance, and inclusion of other instruments like diplomacy, economics, and information to achieve U.S. desired ends and conditions.[1] Joint officers may find themselves involved in the creation or review and revision of a current theater strategy. Combatant Commanders will develop contingency plans (i.e., war plans) as directed by the Chairman's Joint Strategic Campaign Plan These contingency plans will be branches off of the theater campaign plans, and they reside primarily at the Operational Level of warfare.

1   Reveron, Derek S. and Cook, James L. "From National to Theater: Developing Strategy," (Joint Forces Quarterly. Issue 70, 3rd Quarter 2013), 113.

2   Nuechterlein, Donald E. *America Overcommitted: United States National Interests in the 1980s,* (Lexington, KY: The University Press of Kentucky, 1985), 9–10.

3   Nuechterlein, *America Overcommitted,* 9–10.

4   Arthur F. Lykke, Jr., "Toward an Understanding of Military Strategy," chap. in Military Strategy: Theory and Application, (Carlisle Barracks, PA: Department of National Security and Strategy, U.S. Army War College, 1989), 3–8.

5   The Joint Staff. Chairman of the Joint Chiefs Instruction (CJCSI) 3100.01D. *Joint Strategic Planning System (JSPS),* July 20, 2018.

6   CJCSI 3100.01D, *JSPS,* B-1.

7   CJCSI 3100.01D, *JSPS,* B-1.

8   CJCSI 3100.01D, *JSPS,* C-2.

9   CJCSI 3100.01D, *JSPS,* E-1.

10 CJCSI 3100.01D, *JSPS,* F-1

11 CJCSI 3100.01D, *JSPS,* F-2

₁₂ CJCSI 3100.01D, *JSPS*, F-3
₁₃ CJCSI 3100.01D, *JSPS*, G-1
₁₄ CJCSI 3100.01D, *JSPS*, G-1
₁₅ Reveron and Cook, ": Developing Strategy," 116.

CHAPTER 6:
Planning in Joint Organizations

"In preparing for battle, I have always found that plans are useless but planning is indispensable."

— *General of the Army Dwight D. Eisenhower*

General Eisenhower's quote on planning has profound implications for joint planners. When Saddam Hussein and Iraq invaded Kuwait in 1990, General Norman Schwarzkopf indicated that he had a plan for dealing with the invasion and restoring Kuwait's territorial integrity. The implication for the uninformed viewer at the time was that General Schwarzkopf had prepared a master planning document that contained the entire plan for this contingency, and that this document rested on a shelf waiting for an "In case of emergency, just break glass" moment. However, Prussian General Helmuth von Moltke the Elder once famously stated, "No battle plan ever survives first contact with the enemy." All the planners can pour thousands of hours building an ideal plan, but as soon as that plan is finalized, the constantly changing operational environment quickly erodes it into obsolescence. The key for military planners, particularly joint planners, is to realize that planning is a process. Running through this process to create a plan does not mean they have completed the process. Joint and combined organizations will continue to exercise, analyze, and review and refine the plan to account for the constantly changing environment.

Each service and sub-organization has its own planning processes and organizational culture that views planning in different lights. Army officers typically have the strongest background in planning since they have had the Military Decision-Making Process (MDMP) drilled into them from the earliest points in their careers. While each service has its own planning processes, the joint community has the Joint Planning Process (JPP) clearly defined in doctrine that has evolved over the last few decades. The Joint Publication 5-0, Joint Planning defines the "current doctrine in conducting joint, interagency, and multinational planning activities across the range of military operations."[2] Often, officers are assigned to a joint organization without any previous experience or training in the Joint Planning Process. However, once assigned, these officers will often find themselves assigned to solve a problem that requires using the JPP. The Joint Publication 5-0 serves as the "official advice" and guide for how to apply the JPP to solve military problems and develop plans for employing forces to conduct operations.

The Joint Publication 5-0 defines "joint planning" as "the deliberate **process** of determining how (the **ways**) to use military capabilities (the **means**) in time and space to achieve the objectives (the **ends**) while considering the associated **risks**. This is frequently discussed as a method of balancing the ends, ways, and means and identifying where imbalances occur. Those imbalances between the ends, ways, and means define the risks. Commanders only have limited options to address these imbalances. They can redefine the ends or change the objectives to make them more limited, they can request more resources from the Department of Defense, or they can change the ways they use the military capabilities available. Often, senior leaders cannot completely mitigate these imbalances, and when this occurs, they must identify and account for the risks.

Officers typically get an assignment to a joint staff that aligns with their service and area of expertise. A personnel officer will likely go work in the Personnel Directorate (J1). Intelligence officers will typically work in the Intelligence Directorate (J2), and Logistics and Supply officers will work in the Logistics (J4) directorate. Most combat arms specialties (Infantry officers, Surface Warfare Officers, Pilots, etc.) will work in Operations (J3) or Plans Directorate

(J5). Regardless of which Directorate they work in, all joint officers can find themselves pulled in to support an Operational Planning Team (OPT) or a Joint Planning Group (JPG). These teams and groups consist of officers drawn from all directorates and components to work together to solve a command problem and develop a plan. While each service has its respective planning process, the Joint Planning Process (JPP) serves as the primary method for joint planning teams to organize and methodically develop a plan. Ideally, all joint officers would receive their joint education and learn about the Joint Planning Process before they arrive on a joint staff. Unfortunately, many officers don't attend JPME II until a year or two into their joint assignment, and some even wait until the end of their tour to attend this school. As a result, many officers who have minimal joint education and exposure to joint planning find themselves thrust into the role as joint planners, which can feel like trying to board a fast-moving train.

The Joint Planning Process is a seven-step process that runs from Planning Initiation to Plan or Order Development (see Figure 9). The Joint Publication 5-0 defines the JPP as "**an orderly, analytical set of logical steps to frame a problem; examine a mission; develop, analyze, and compare alternate courses of action (COAs); select the best COA; and produce a plan or order.**"[3] While at first glance it appears fairly simple, each of those seven steps consists of complex analyses and processes, and can have many steps embedded within them. A planning team given a problem to solve can find themselves spending weeks on just the Mission Analysis step to build a solid foundation on which the remainder of the JPP rests. The JPP offers key touchpoints with the commander when the joint planning group will present their analysis and products to the commander for consideration, further guidance, and hopefully, approval.

Figure 9: Joint Planning Process

Joint Planning Process

Step 1	Planning Initiation
Step 2	Mission Analysis
Step 3	Course of Action (COA) Development
Step 4	COA Analysis and Wargaming
Step 5	COA Comparison
Step 6	COA Approval
Step 7	Plan or Order Development

Figure V-1. Joint Planning Process

Source: Joint Staff, "Joint Publication 5-0, Joint Planning"

Planning Initiation marks the beginning of the process, and "begins when an appropriate authority recognizes the potential for military capability to be employed in support of national objectives or in response to a potential or actual crisis."[4] This can occur when the President or Secretary of Defense notifies the Combatant Commander to develop a plan and options to deal with a particular problem, or it can come from the Commander proactively recognizing that a potential problem is emerging that may require a plan to address.[5] Once the Commander deems the need for a planning effort, the staff will convene a planning team to begin the planning process. This leads to officers from across the staff to leave their day-to-day staff jobs and become part of a JPG. Early in this planning process, the planning team members should review strategic guidance documents like the National Security Strategy, National Defense Strategy, National Military Strategy, Joint Strategic Campaign Plan, and any planning guidance they received from the commander or the Joint Staff. This will serve to set the team and ensure their planning begins with the higher national policy in mind.

Mission Analysis follows planning initiation. This is the most involved step in the Joint Planning Process and requires detailed thought and planning from the group. The Mission Analysis step alone can take weeks, depending on how long the planning team has to develop the plan. While most officers new to joint planning want to immediately try to solve the problem and develop options, they need to slow down and realize that a thorough mission analysis will take significant time and effort and forms the foundation for developing a successful plan. Mission Analysis consists of more than a dozen steps by itself. It begins with analyzing the strategic guidance further, ensuring a clear understanding of the commander's initial planning guidance, which includes timelines, level of detail required in the plan, and intent. The planning team will seek to define and understand the operational environment, including relevant actors, geographic considerations, tendencies, and potentials. Reviewing higher headquarters guidance for facts and assumptions, the planning team will identify key facts and assumptions. Assumptions are those educated estimates of the situation that they require to continue planning. In the interim, the intelligence personnel will seek to gather information that will either validate those assumptions and turn them into known facts, or invalidate them as untrue. The planning team can then add those validated assumptions to their facts list, or remove the invalid assumptions and adjust their analysis to account for those changes. The team will develop an initial operational approach, which includes a summary of the current conditions, the desired end state, the problem definition, and broad lines of operation and lines of effort for taking the current conditions, solving the problem, and reaching the desired ends.

The final product of Mission Analysis will consist of a briefing to the commander that seeks to gain approval for the commander's critical information requirements (CCIRs), the task list (specified, implied, and essential tasks), and a mission statement that includes the Who, What, Where, When, and Why for the plan. The Who will be the joint or combined task force or the command. The What part of the mission statement will include the essential tasks that must occur for mission accomplishment. The Why describes the purpose of the plan and most often follows the words "in order to." The

When and Where typically explain that this plan will commence "On order" or "When directed" and state the location or provide a general "in the Joint Operating Area." Figure 10 illustrates an example of a mission statement that includes all of the five "Ws." While officers want to jump to the "How" and develop options, they first need to identify the 5 Ws and lay this foundation for successful course of action development. The team will develop the "How" in the next steps of the planning process.

Figure 10: Example Mission Statement

EXAMPLE MISSION STATEMENT

When directed [when], United States X Command, in concert with coalition partners [who] deters Country Y from coercing its neighbors and proliferating weapons of mass destruction [what] in order to maintain security [why] in the region [where].

Source: Joint Publication 5-0, "Joint Planning"

Figure 11 shows a sample outline for a Mission Analysis briefing offered in the Joint Publication 5-0. This offers a good checklist for planners to use to ensure they complete all the steps of Mission Analysis, present the appropriate information to the Commander and senior staff, and ensure they get review and approval on the required items before transitioning to the next steps in the Joint Planning Process. Even when planners have completed Mission Analysis, they must continually monitor the operational environment, including the review of updated strategic guidance, to ensure their Mission Analysis still holds. Changes in the world situation or in the Commander's Area of Responsibility may change facts or assumptions, or could alter the tasks and end states. While we have a strong tendency to want to mark a step complete and put it in the rearview mirror, the planning effort and final plan will be far better served if the planning team revisits Mission Analysis and adjusts those outputs first before altering the courses of action or the final plan. Another key item the staff will want to develop during this step is the initial Course of Action evaluation criteria. These will prove vital later in the process when developing and selecting a course of action for the final plan.

Example Mission Analysis Briefing

- Introduction
- Situation overview
  - Operational environment (including joint operations area) and threat overview
  - Political, military, economic, social, information, and infrastructure strengths and weaknesses
  - Enemy (including center[s] of gravity) and objectives
- Friendly assessment
  - Facts and assumptions
  - Limitations—constraints/restraints
  - Capabilities allocated
  - Legal considerations
- Communication synchronization
- Objectives, effects, and task analysis
  - United States Government interagency objectives
  - Higher commander's objectives/mission/guidance
  - Objectives and effects
  - Specified/implied/essential tasks
  - Centers of gravity
- Operational protection
  - Operational risk
  - Mitigation
- Proposed initial commander's critical information requirements
- Mission
  - Proposed mission statement
  - Proposed commander's intent
- Command relationships
- Conclusion—potential resource shortfalls
- Mission analysis approval and commander's course of action planning guidance

Figure V-6. Example Mission Analysis Briefing

Source: Joint Publication 5-0, "Joint Planning"

Once Mission Analysis has concluded and the Commander has approved the products, the planners can proceed to developing options. These options must meet the intent of the Mission Statement and accomplish the required tasks. However, there will be many ways the military can solve the problem. Taking the Mission Analysis products and any Commander's guidance, the planners will begin developing the "How" through Course of Action (COA)

Development. Joint Pub 5-0 defines a Course of Action as "a potential way (solution, method) to accomplish the assigned mission."[6] Before diving in to developing these options, planners need to understand the difference between validity criteria and selection criteria. Each COA the staff develops must be a valid option. Valid means the option is Adequate, Feasible, Distinguishable, Acceptable, and Complete (AFDAC). An **adequate** option will accomplish the mission, meet the commander's intent, accomplish all essential tasks, and achieve the desired end state.[7] A **feasible** option can accomplish the mission within the time allotted and within resource limitations.[8] **Distinguishable** options mean that the courses of action developed differ significantly from each other so that the commander actually has a distinct choice between them. Two distinguishable COAs will have different focus or direction of their main effort, a scheme of maneuver, task organization, and a different primary mechanism for mission accomplishment.[9] An **acceptable** option will not include unacceptable risks and fits within the strategic objectives.[10] Finally, a **complete** COA will answer the questions who, what, where, when, how, and why; and has all the required elements including the major forces required, concepts for deployment, employment, and sustainment; and clearly defines the end state and mission success criteria. Courses of Action that don't check all five of these criteria are not valid. The planning team must develop at least two valid Courses of Action for consideration and selection.

Once the Joint Planning Group has created and thoroughly developed their valid courses of action, they need to prepare a second briefing to the Commander to ensure the options meet his guidance. The Course of Action briefing simply presents the two or three options to the Commander, but these must be valid and fully developed courses of action. Typically, the joint planning team will divide up into two or three separate COA Teams to independently develop their different options. Each COA will have a COA sketch showing broadly how that option will accomplish the mission statement, and it will break down each COA by phases. Earlier versions of joint doctrine defined operations as five-phased endeavors (Deter, Seize the Initiative, Dominate, Stabilize, and Enable Transition to Civil Authorities). However, most joint organizations took this phase model as directive guidance and developed all plans based on that five-phased construct. The most recent joint doctrine simply states that courses of action will have phases, but it broadly labels the phases as pre-conflict, conflict, and post-conflict, leaving it to the Commanders to decide what phases and how many phases they need to accomplish the mission. For the COA briefing, each COA will have phases, and these phases may be determined during Mission Analysis. During the COA briefing, the teams will develop a sketch for each phase that includes the task organization including a command and control chart showing who will command the operation, who will lead the components (land, sea, air, space, etc.), and what tasks each component will perform during each phase. The COA Briefing will result in the Commander seeing all of the options developed, finalize the COA selection criteria, and gain approval for the planners to proceed to analyzing and wargaming the courses of action before moving to comparison and finally selecting the best option.

The planning team will also want to refine COA Comparison criteria and the comparison methodology during this phase. Ideally, they would have some initial proposed comparison criteria developed in the Mission Analysis step, prior to COA Development. The team will definitely want to fully develop and agree on those criteria before they begin to analyze and wargame the options. A good practice would include offering draft comparison criteria as part of the Mission Analysis briefing to the commander, so the senior leaders have an opportunity to review, consider, and even make inputs to those criteria. The team could include a refined list of these comparison criteria and the proposed comparison methodology during the COA briefing. Fully developing the comparison criteria early, before COA Analysis and Wargaming, will help avert strong disagreements between planners who become emotionally attached to their courses of action they have invested significant time and energy into developing.

Once the commander has seen the COAs, the planners will conduct wargaming to test the options against the adversary. A common way to conduct wargaming is to select a few planners to act as the adversary, the Red Team. One or two senior planners will act as the impartial White Cell that will referee the wargame and adjudicate any disputes. Finally, members of each COA team will act as the friendly forces Blue Team. There are many methods for conducting a wargame, and each joint organization will have its own unique processes. The key point to understand here is that planners will run each COA separately through the wargame, and the team will appoint recorders to capture notes for each phase of the operation the team simulates. These notes will become an important input for the next step, COA Comparison.

The Joint Planning doctrine unambiguously states that "COAs are not compared with each other within any one criterion, but rather they're individually evaluated against the criteria that are established by the staff and commander."[11] A real-world example for this would be a family moving to a new assignment. When they go to the new location, they will need to find a home to live in. It's easy to get bogged down in trying to compare multiple homes to each other. The COA Comparison methodology can apply to this real-world example. When posed to a JPME II Seminar, we ask what do you look for in a home. Common responses are size, distance from the base (i.e., commute time), quality of schools, house price, access to shopping, and a myriad of other criteria. A family with children will consider the quality of schools as a top priority criterion. Another family with no children likely won't consider schools important but will want to live closer to shopping and dining venues. The point is for each individual family to write down their criteria, rank those criteria either from number 1 through X, extremely important to less important, or some other scale that works. Once these criteria are defined, it will be easier to find some suitable homes (valid COAs) and apply those criteria to each home independently and determine which one rates highest.

Similarly, joint planners can develop comparison criteria for their COAs. They can determine whether all the criteria are equal or if some are more important than others and should carry more weight. The team can decide whether they want to use a non-numerical method, a numerical method, or a weighted numerical method. Once the team has determined what criteria they will use and what methodology to use, it's critical to run each Course of Action independently through the criteria, determine the advantages and disadvantages or scores. Defining the criteria and methodology before comparison will reduce arguments between COA team members who feel a need to defend their options they have invested significant time and effort into developing and wargaming. Once the team has completed COA comparison, they can prepare the Course of Action Recommendation briefing to the Commander and seek a final decision.

Step 6, COA Selection involves the planning team briefing their Courses of Action, their comparison criteria and methodology, and the results of analysis and comparison, which will conclude with a recommended option to the Commander. The briefing can go different ways. The Commander can agree with the recommendation and take that option as the basis for final plan development. The Commander can disagree with the COA recommendation and choose a different option. Often, the Commander will like aspects of multiple options presented and directing the planning team to develop and refine a blended course of action. If that's the case, the planning team will go back to the COA Development step, create a blended option, conduct wargaming and analysis as required to ensure the option will work and identify risks, and present this final COA back to the Commander. Once the Commander has approved a course of action, the planning team can proceed to the seventh and final step if the Joint Planning Process, Plan or Order Development.

At this point, planners may feel like they have approached the proverbial finish line. However, taking all of the products from Mission Analysis and Course of Action Development and selection and converting that into a Plan or Order document involves significant work. Joint Publication 5-0 states that "in most cases, the directive will be standardized in the five-paragraph format," which includes Situation, Mission, Execution, Administration & Logistics, and Command and Control (C2). Situation and Mission will often be short paragraphs, with the Mission consisting of only the approved Mission Statement developed during Mission Analysis. Paragraph 3, Execution, will describe in detail by phase of the operation what each component will do. Providing all of these details so subordinate components (land, sea, air, space, special operations, etc.) will take extensive writing and can make many of these plans fill hundreds of pages depending the level of detail required. Administration & Logistics will cover how the forces will deploy and how the organization will sustain those forces throughout the operation. Command & Control will describe with organizational charts who will lead the operation, who will lead the components, and how the United States forces will work with other nations and the control arrangements that will apply and change throughout each phase.

Joint Planning is a deeply involved process and taxing endeavor. Depending on the situation, joint officers could have weeks or months to plan, or they may have to run through the planning process very quickly and produce options within a few days. Officers who have never had exposure to the Joint Planning Process, either through real-world or exercise planning efforts or through JPME II, will likely feel lost the first time they experience it. Reading through the Joint Publication 5-0 Chapter V will provide a good initial understanding, and this document serves as a valuable reference during the planning process, even for highly experienced planners.

1   Reveron and Cook, ": Developing Strategy," 116.

2   The Joint Staff. "Joint Planning," (Washington DC: Joint Publication 5-0, 2017),

3   The Joint Staff, Joint Publication 5-0, V-1.

4   The Joint Staff, Joint Publication 5-0, V-4.

5   The Joint Staff, Joint Publication 5-0, V-4.

6   The Joint Staff, Joint Publication 5-0, V-20.

7   The Joint Staff, Joint Publication 5-0, V-28.

8   The Joint Staff, Joint Publication 5-0, V-28.

9   The Joint Staff, Joint Publication 5-0, V-29.

10 The Joint Staff, Joint Publication 5-0, V-29.

11 The Joint Staff, Joint Publication 5-0, V-43.

CHAPTER 7:
Managing Human Talent in a Joint Organization

The first step to managing human talent in a joint organization involves understanding the structure of the organization. Most joint headquarters organizations follow the standard hierarchical staff structure that officers become familiar within their respective Service. While staff directorates have a "G" designation for "Ground" in an Army or Marine headquarters, the Navy uses "N" and the Air Force "A" for Naval and Air staff, respectively. Joint organizations use "J" for joint, but the numbers remain the same. Like a G1 or A1 directorate, the J1 is the Personnel directorate. J2 is Intelligence, J3 Operations, J4 Logistics, J5 Plans, and so on. Officers in career fields, making them specifically Personnelists, Intelligence, or Logistics officers, will commonly work in those directorates. Most joint assignees from operational career fields will work in the J3 Operations or J5 Plans directorates. Depending on their rank and experience, these officers can either work in a division and branch within those directorates (e.g., J33 Current Operations, J39 Information Operations, etc.). More senior officers such as senior O4 and O5s can enter as Branch Chiefs, and Colonels and Navy Captains will typically run Divisions.

It's important to realize that officers filling JDAL positions come to the joint organization at crucial points in their careers. As soon as officers are selected for Field Grade (Major, Lieutenant Commander), they have opportunities ("looks") for boards to review their record every year for either appropriate level service schools, command screening boards, and promotion boards. Often, two or more of these events occur each year, and it is incumbent on the officer to know about these events and plan for them. The Air Force's Air Mobility Command developed a good mentoring tool called a "Ribbon Chart" (Figure 12) to help officers track these events. While this tool is specific to the Air Force, it applies to officers from all the services who face similar cascading milestones between the 10-year and 20-year career point. As a supervisor leading joint officers, encourage them to create their own ribbon chart specific to them individually and use it as a tool to both learn about them and their career goals and timelines, while also encouraging them to take increased ownership of their careers. The example Ribbon Chart in Figure 12 applies for an Air Force officer commissioned in 2003. Block 2 has what their Developmental Team Vector for their career field offered. In this case, the officer has a Developmental Team vector to progress to Headquarters Air Force (HAF). Block 4 is this officer's Air Force Specialty Code (11/12M for a pilot).

Figure 12: Air Force Officer Ribbon Chart

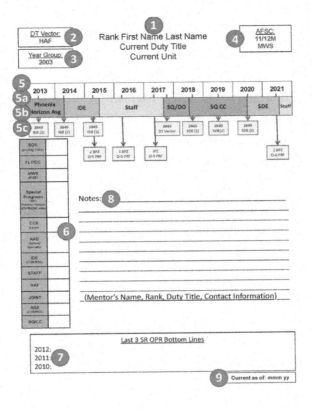

Source: Major Chris Stephens, "A Mighty Mentoring Tool"

Major Chris Stephens described the Ribbon Chart in his 2013 article titled "A Mighty Mentoring Tool" as "a personalized development plan offering a visual representation of an individual's past, present, and future experiences."[2] As seen in the example of an Air Force officer commissioned in 2003, key career milestone events begin occurring at the 10-year point with the first of three annual looks for Intermediate Developmental Education (IDE). In conjunction with their third and final opportunity for intermediate school, the officer has the first of three looks for their next promotion. Each of these annual promotion boards requires the officer and their supervisor to prepare a Promotion Recommendation Form (PRF) that goes to the promotion board. Not shown in this example ribbon chart are the four opportunities to screen for command at the 15, 16, 17, and 18-year points. The officer will then have three opportunities for Senior Developmental Education (SDE) and then, if they are eligible, beginning hitting their first promotion opportunities to O6 at the 18-year point. This example focuses on an Air Force officer's career, but officers from all services will face a similar timeline for service school selection, command selection, and promotion opportunities. The important point for a joint leader is to encourage all their officers to create a similar map and determine their individual aspirations and what they need during their joint tour to ensure they continue to progress when they return to their respective service.

The bottom block with the last three senior rater Officer Performance Report (OPR) bottom lines is probably the most important for the Air Force officer. Chapter 8 will go in-depth on how to complete annual appraisals for officers from the four services. This block contains the bottom line from the Senior Rater block on each of the officer's last three OPRs. This ensures consistency in the officer's record and gives a view of what the trend shows. When you rate on Air Force officers as their Rater, you will have six lines to record their performance over the rating period. The sixth line is the most important line since the stratifications and command push (e.g., "Sq/CC soonest!") in this line often go into the officer's promotion recommendation. Even more vital is the Senior Rater's block. The Senior Rater gets four lines, and their bottom line will also have a stratification and push statement. Highlighting the last three in the Ribbon Chart will help facilitate the mentoring process, give the supervisor a sense of where the officer they're supervising lies in terms of future potential, and enables an open discussion on what near-term opportunities the officer should seek during their joint assignment.

Command Selection

Command selection will be one of the most pivotal points in a military officer's career. While some Army officers get to serve as platoon commanders and company commanders early in their career, Air Force officers lead as Flight commanders, and Navy officers as section heads, command at the O5 (Lieutenant Colonel/Commander) level is the strongest determinant into whether an officer will continue to advance beyond that level. Most officers only get two or three windows to compete for these coveted command opportunities, and many times these windows will coincide with the officers' tour in a joint organization. Each Service employs very different processes and timelines for selecting its officers for O5-level command opportunities. The Air Force uses the Airman Development Plan (ADP) website to nominate officers for assignment, developmental education, and command consideration. The Marine Corps uses its standard assignment process, and officers select battalion or squadron command openings among their assignment choices. The Navy uses a command screening board that reviews officer records and selects them for command at a predetermined point in their careers.[3] The Army first implemented its Battalion Commanders Assessment Program (BCAP) in 2020, with the first iterations running in January through February 2020.

Some Army officers half-jokingly refer to BCAP as the Army's "Hunger Games." West Point's Modern War Institute describes the Army's new Battalion Commander Assessment Program (BCAP) as the "Army's NFL Combine."[4] After years of issues with toxic leaders, the Army appointed the Army Talent Management Task Force (ATMTF) to study the critical question of the best way to select the Army's future battalion commanders.[5] According to Everett Spain's article, the BCAP seeks to achieve three major effects on the Army. First, it will help identify toxic leaders and screen them from taking command. Second, it will allow officers who may not make it to the top from impersonal selection boards to rise in the rankings and earn command opportunities. Third, The Army seeks to fundamentally change the Army officer corps' organizational culture to more deeply value critical and innovative thinking, effective oral and written communication, strategic temperament, and authentic respect for subordinates and peers.[6] BCAP involves battalion command candidates traveling to Fort Leavenworth, Kansas for four-day sessions. Upon arrival, the candidates take the Army's Personal Fitness Test and have their height and weight measured. Candidates who failed this portion were eliminated from contention and sent home. The remainder of BCAP consists of officers taking "a series of cognitive, non-cognitive, physical, verbal, and written assessments."[7] The BCAP concludes with a blind interview with a panel of senior Army officers.[8] Candidates have moved up or down the battalion commander selection list based on the results of the first rounds of BCAP, and the Army published the first battalion commander selection list based on this process in late March 2020.

Recognition Programs

Recognition of personnel for their performance is a morale booster and can encourage people to work hard and seek opportunities. Most joint headquarters have a Quarterly and Annual awards program. These usually include a Junior Enlist Member, Noncommissioned Officer (NCO), Senior NCO, Company Grade Officer (CGO), and Field Grade Officer (FGO) of the Quarter and Year categories. Civilian Employees can also qualify for Civilian of the Quarter and Year awards categories. Each joint organization will have its unique process, but typically this requires the supervisor working with the individual to keep up with their professional accomplishments, self-improvement activities, and community involvement. Quarters run January–March, April–June, July–September, and October–December. To ensure timely recognition, many organizations require supervisors to complete their nomination forms and submit them as much as a month before the end of the quarter. Annual Award nominations are often due in December to allow the command to convene boards to review the forms and decide the award winners in time to present these awards to the recipients near the beginning of the next quarter or year.

While completing these nomination forms may seem burdensome, the process also gives supervisors the opportunity to exercise their writing skills, and encourages staff officers to track and record their accomplishments. Having this record makes it much easier when the supervisor has to complete the annual appraisal forms on their officers and civilian personnel. Having a rate receive a Quarterly or Annual award also makes a much stronger case for a top-level stratification statement on their performance report. A major winning a Field Grade Officer of the Year award for a Directorate consisting of 120 officers can legitimately claim a "#1/120 Field Grade Officers" for the year on their fitness report, which can have a tremendous positive impact when they compete for school, command, or promotion.

Another way supervisors can recognize their personnel includes nominating them for Joint decorations when they have a major accomplishment. The U.S. Transportation Command's Joint Enabling Capabilities Command (JECC) supports Combatant Command exercises and typically sends teams of 10-20 officers to support those exercises. The JECC will select an officer to serve as the exercise team lead. This officer attends the Initial, Mid, and Final Planning Conferences, coordinates with the Command for how many people they need and what kinds of expertise, and settles the travel and lodging arrangements. This exercise team lead also ensures that the personnel participating in the exercise have the required training. He briefs the JECC leaders on the status and leads the team overseas to participate in the one or two-week exercise. When the team returns, the exercise team lead gathers the lessons learned and provides an out brief to the JECC Commander. This exercise team leader gains tremendous experience in terms of project management, joint leadership, planning, and briefing skills from this endeavor. When these exercise teams do well, the JECC will often recognize the team leader with a joint decoration (e.g., Joint Service Achievement Medal) and present it to them through a public recognition event each quarter. This decoration and the associated citation will go into the officer's permanent personnel record as well, so all future boards will see it when considering that officer for command or promotion opportunities.

Hiring

Occasionally, a joint leader may have to hire civilian personnel. This will happen more often in overseas joint organizations where civilians may fill a position for three or four years before moving back to the United States. The Civilian Personnel office in the J1 will help significantly with this process, but the joint officer will often find themselves designated as the hiring authority to fill the position. The first step will be to review the civilian position description and update it as needed to ensure the new civilian hired will have the required qualifications and education to successfully perform the job. Next, the hiring official will have to advertise the job. The Department of Defense fills most civilian jobs by advertising them on the www.USAJobs.gov website. The hiring official will fill out the form required that they can obtain from the Civilian Personnel office. Once completed and turned in, the Civilian Personnel office will advertise the job and screen applications eligible prospects. Typically, after four to eight weeks, the hiring official will receive the list of eligible applicants and their Federal job resumes. Every state and location has different rules, but the most common will involve the hiring official reviewing the eligible applicants and making a selection based on the most qualified candidate.

My experience with this process involved filling three GS-12 positions at Headquarters Air Mobility Command. For the first position, I had "Direct Hire Authority" to find a qualified individual and make a direct job offer. Once this was done, the Civilian Personnel office handled the details for in-processing the new hire. The second position went through the standard job advertisement process. Hundreds of people applied for the job. The Office of Personnel Management (OPM) screened the applications for keywords and provided 63 resumes of fully qualified applicants. Feeling overwhelmed, I picked some key personnel from my branch, and we each individually read through the resumes. I told each of them to pick their "Top 5" based on the qualifications. After this, we came together and agreed on who the Top 5 applicants were based on their resumes and the position we were trying to fill. At this point, we could have made a selection as each of these individuals was fully qualified for the position. However, interviewing the candidates offers the best chance to meet the individuals and assess how they will fit into the organization.

Most bases have a rule that the hiring official can interview all, some, or none of their potential candidates. When I received 63 federal resumes, I decided to pare this list down to a top 10, and then further refine it to a Top 5 candidates that we would call for interviews. Having never conducted an interview before as a hiring official, I talked to several mentors and even purchased books to help learn how to interview. What we decided in our branch was to come up with 10–12 standard questions and hold a three-person hiring panel to conduct the interview. We developed and agreed on the questions we would ask and even rehearsed the order in which we would ask the questions and which member of the panel would ask each question. During the interview, we each took notes on the candidates' responses and our impressions and scored the responses to the interview questions. After each interview, we conferred and discussed our findings and scores. After completing all of the interviews, we conferred and decided which candidates were our first choice, second choice, and third choice. The final step was to submit our hiring selection to the Civilian Personnel office. Once submitted, that process is completely out of the hiring official's hands. The Civilian Personnel office and OPM will make the job offer to the first choice, negotiate salary, and coordinate the new employee's start date. If for any reason, the first-choice candidate and the Civilian Personnel office cannot reach agreement they will then extend the job offer to the second-choice candidate and so on.

Many officers assigned to a joint organization will never deal with the civilian hiring process during their joint assignment. However, it's at least something they should consider, so they won't start from a dead stop trying to prepare for this process. At some point in an officer's career, whether during the joint tour or later when they fill command positions or more senior positions on headquarters staff organization, they most likely will have to participate in a hiring action as either a hiring official or as a member of an interviewing panel that will make recommendations on who to hire.

Joint Qualified Officers

Services send their officers to joint assignments, and specifically to JDAL billets, to make them Joint Qualified Officers (JQOs). As mentioned, officers must fulfill two requirements to earn the JQO designation. First, they must complete the requisite time in a Joint Duty assignment. Historically this has meant 36 months. However, the Services can waive this down to 22 months, and frequently will do this for an officer that they need to move early for command or education opportunities. Officers can also earn time by filling joint positions during short deployments such as individual augmentees to Iraq, Afghanistan, or other overseas locations. The second requirement for JQO designation is earning JPME II credit. Most officers receive this by attending the ten-week residence program in Norfolk. Ideally, officers would attend JPME II either en route to their joint assignment or within their first year. Unfortunately, many commands only send their officers in their last year. The result is that officers arrive and spend their joint tours without the benefit of formally learning the national strategy-making processes or the joint planning processes. Joint leaders can help change this trend by pushing for their officers to attend JPME II either en route or within the first year of their joint tour so they can apply this knowledge, and the joint or combined organization can reap the benefits. Sending officers early in their joint tour represents an investment of both funding and time. Sending them near the end of their tour fosters a "checking the box" mentality and minimizes the benefit to the joint organizations.

1   Stephens, Major Chris. "A Mighty Mentoring Tool," *Air Force News,* May 29, 2013, https://www.mcchord.af.mil/News/Commentaries/Display/Article/248524/a-mighty-mentoring-tool.

2   Stephens, Major Chris. "A Mighty Mentoring Tool," May 29, 2013.

3   Interview with CDR Derek Fix, USN, February 20, 2020.

4   Spain, Everett. "The Army's NFL Combine: The Battalion Commander Assessment Program" *Modern War Institute at West Point*, January 12, 2020, mwi.usma.edu/armys-nfl-combine-battalion-commander-assessment-program.

5   Spain, "The Army's NFL Combine,"

6   Spain. "The Army's NFL Combine."

7   Department of the Army, Army Talent Management Task Force, "Battalion Commander Assessment Program," *Army.mil, December 6, 2019,* www.Army.mil/standto/archive_2019-12-06

8   Army Talent Management Task Force, "Battalion Commander Assessment Program."

CHAPTER 8:
Assessing and Evaluating Talent in Joint Organizations

Conducting supervision and annual appraisals of military personnel will be your most important task as a joint leader. Officers assigned to joint duty typically arrive between their 12 and 16-year point in service, and they usually reside in a joint position for three years. They will have three annual performance reports in their records upon departure which represents as much as 20% of their entire career personnel record. These reports can make or break an officer's career, depending on how they're written.

When officers arrive at a joint assignment, they are usually well-versed in their own respective service's performance appraisal system and know what verbiage resonates and what doesn't with promotion boards and command selection boards. However, these officers have likely never seen a performance report from any of the other services, and they typically receive no training on how to rate officers from other services. The officer evaluation forms vary significantly from one service to the next, and even have different names. An Army officer receives an Officer Evaluation Report (AER). Air Force officers receive an Officer Performance Report (OPR). Naval officers and Marines get an annual Fitness Report (FITREP), but even these two services have very disparate forms and processes for their personnel. The Air Force broke out from the Army in

1947. Prior to that point, Air Force officers were Army Air Forces officers and had the same performance appraisals as all other Army officers. Since that split, the officer appraisal systems of the services have evolved very differently. On December 20, 2019, with the creation of the US Space Force, space officers from the Air Force will detach and become part of this newest service. For now, the annual Officer Performance Reports will remain the same. Over time however, the evaluations for Air Force and Space Force officers will diverge as well.

Army Officer Evaluation Report (OER)

Army Regulation 623-3 (AR 623-3), Personnel Evaluation, Evaluation Reporting System, governs how Army personnel are rated. To be eligible for an Officer Evaluation report (OER), "a Soldier will complete 90 calendar days in the same position under the same rater."[1] However, normally an OER will cover a 12-month rating period of performance. For any Soldier receiving an Evaluation Report, there are three key individuals in the rating chain and directly involved in the process: The rated Soldier, the rater (i.e. immediate supervisor), and the senior rater (i.e., the supervisor's rater). Each of these three individuals bears particular responsibilities in the evaluation process.

The AR 623-3 states that "The rated Soldier is the subject of the evaluation and has considerable responsibility in the evaluation process."[2] "Within 30 days after the beginning of each new rating period and at least quarterly thereafter," the rated Soldier must participate in counseling and discuss with the rater the duty description, performance objectives, and academic standards as appropriate.[3] Additionally, rated Soldiers must complete an evaluation support form with their rater in which they "assess (with the rater) the validity of objectives or compliance with academic standards throughout the rating period."[4] While this system seems bureaucratically onerous, it does serve to ensure both the rated Soldier and the rating official establish an agreed-upon benchmark of expectations and continual feedback throughout the rating period leading up to the final evaluation report. Army officers who report to a joint organization will expect this process, and officers from other services who find themselves rating on Army officers need awareness of this process so they can effectively supervise and lead those Soldiers.

The rater also has significant responsibilities outlined in the Army Regulation. The rater must "provide a copy of their support form, along with the senior rater's support form, to the rated Soldier receiving an OER at the beginning of the rating period."[5] The rater must meet with the rated Soldier within 30 days of the start of the rating period to discuss the scope of the Soldier's duty description and the performance objectives to maintain.[6] Additionally, raters should describe how the individual's duty description and objectives relate "with the organization's mission, problems, priorities, and similar matters."[7] For a joint organization, this starts with understanding the joint organization's mission, priorities, and goals. Since most joint officers will work below the directorate level, and in a staff branch, this discussion will begin with laying out the branch's mission and priorities, tying those to the higher Directorate goals, and nest those within the overall joint organization's mission, vision, and priorities. Near the end of the rating period, the rater will use the support forms and the Army Officer Evaluation Report (OER) form "to provide an accurate assessment of the rated Soldier's performance and potential (as applicable)" on the evaluation report.[8]

Senor Raters also play a key role in the evaluation process and determining the officer's future in the Army. "Senior raters or reviewing officials use their positions and experiences to evaluate the rated Soldier's performance and/or potential within a broad organizational perspective."[9] The AR 623-3 further states that "the senior rater's evaluation is the link between the day-to-day observation of the rated Soldier and the longer-term evaluation of the Soldier's potential" by the Army's selection boards which determine officer promotions and select officers for key command positions. The senior rater serves as the final reviewer of the OER before the rated officer signs the form and it goes into their permanent personnel record as a final document.

The Department of the Army's OER form (DA Form 67-10-2) (Figure 13) is the standard form across the Army for all officers, and those assigned to supervise Army officers at a joint organization will use this standardized form to evaluate all Army officers. The first page of this two-page form is relatively standard. It has blocks to enter identifying information for the rated Soldier, the rater, and the senior rater. The organization information and Soldier's duties and responsibilities, developed and coordinated on the evaluation support form, also go here. The first opportunity to comment on the Soldier's future potential is at the bottom section, Part IV. The rater and senior rater can add recommendations for future broadening assignments in block b, and for future Army assignments and command consideration in block c. The final block allows for a comment on the rated officer's character. The AR 623-3 states that all comments on the form "will not exceed the space provided on the evaluation reports" and these comments also "must pertain exclusively to the rating period of the evaluation report."[10] Additionally, the Army Regulation prohibits certain narrative techniques like bullet comments or any technique used to make specific words stand out from the rest of the narrative such as underlining, italics, excessive quotation marks, and the like.[11] Finally, raters shall not include "inappropriate references to box checks" or "specific selection board-type language."[12]

Figure 13: Sample Army Officer Evaluation Report (OER), Page 1

FIELD GRADE PLATE (O4 - O5; CW3 - CW5) OFFICER EVALUATION REPORT — See Privacy Act Statement in AR 623-3.

For use of this form, see AR 623-3; the proponent agency is DCS, G-1.

PART I - ADMINISTRATIVE (Rated Officer)

RANK: MAJ DATE OF RANK (YYYYMMDD): 20130601 BRANCH: AD

UNIT, ORG., STATION, ZIP CODE OR APO, MAJOR COMMAND: HQ Allied Rapid Reaction Corps, Imjin Barracks/PSC38, 09403, JJ

UIC: W2HW01 REASON FOR SUBMISSION: 02 Annual

PERIOD COVERED: FROM (YYYYMMDD) 20160504 THRU (YYYYMMDD) 20170503 RATED MONTHS: 12 NO. OF ENCLOSURES: 0

PART II - AUTHENTICATION

RANK: COL POSITION: Chief Info Ops/CoS JEC DATE: 20170711

RANK: BG POSITION: Deputy Chief of Staff-Ops

SENIOR RATER'S ORGANIZATION: HQ, Allied Rapid Reaction Corps-UK BRANCH: GO COMPONENT: RA

SENIOR RATER PHONE NUMBER: (314) 236-8830 DATE: 20170713 DATE: 20170714

This is a referred report, do you wish to make comments? [ ] Referral [ ] Yes, comments are attached [ ] No

Supplementary Review Required? [ ] Yes [X] No

MSAF Date (YYYYMMDD): 20160321

PART III - DUTY DESCRIPTION

PRINCIPAL DUTY TITLE: SO2 AMD Plans Coordinator POSITION AOC/BRANCH: 14A/AD

SIGNIFICANT DUTIES AND RESPONSIBILITIES: Senior air and missile defense and airspace management planner in a joint and multi-national North Atlantic Treaty Organization Headquarters, required to rapidly deploy anywhere in the world in support of NATO operations. Plans and coordinates the operational requirements and placement of multi-national air defense units for the NATO Allied Rapid Reaction Corps consisting of more than 400 personnel. Critical member of operational planning groups with a secondary role of performing duties in the Joint Operations Center as necessary. Serves as the executive officer for the United States contingent of the ARRC. Responsible for assisting the Senior National Representative for the operational readiness of the U.S. Servicemen and Families assigned to this 3-star joint and multi-national headquarters.

PART IV - PERFORMANCE EVALUATION - PROFESSIONALISM, COMPETENCIES, AND ATTRIBUTES (Rater)

APFT Pass/Fail/Profile: PASS Date: 20170328 Height: 73 Weight: 196 Within Standard? YES

THIS OFFICER POSSESSES SKILLS AND QUALIFIES FOR THE FOLLOWING BROADENING ASSIGNMENTS: CSA Initiatives Group, Congressional Liaison, Fellowship

THIS OFFICER POSSESSES SKILLS AND QUALIFIES FOR THE FOLLOWING OPERATIONAL ASSIGNMENTS: BN Commander, BDE DCO, BDE Commander

Character: MAJ XXX is an impressive officer of solid character. He is forthright and full of candor. He lives the Army Values and the Warrior Ethos. Strong supporter of EO, EEO and SHARP. He is disciplined but also is empathetic in his focus on mission and people.

DA FORM 67-10-2, NOV 2015

Page 1 of 2

Source: LTC John Doe, "Sample Army Officer Evaluation Report"

Page 2 of the OER (Figure 14) allows raters and senior raters to begin assessing the officer's performance during the rating period. Block IV, d2 offers guidance on narrative comments, and in the example, this narrative clearly does not consist of bullet comments crafted to fill all of the white space in the block. The rater provides a rating on the Soldier in Block e (Fig. 14) and provides final narrative-style comments. Particular to the Army is the creation of a rater profile and a senior rater profile. "The rater must have less than 50 percent of the ratings of each rank in the "Excels" box.[13] The Army controls these rater profiles electronically, and the AR 623-3 states that if a rater submits an OER with an "Excels" rating "that causes a rater's profile to have 50 percent or more "Excels" ratings," then that OER will be processed with a "Proficient" Headquarters, Department of the Army (HQDA) electronically generated label.[14] Army officers know this and try to carefully manage their individual rater profiles to ensure they remain below that 50 percent. Army officers often refer to these "Excels" and "Proficient" ratings as "Above Center of Mass" and "Center of Mass."

Similarly, senior raters also build a profile which limits the number of "Most Qualified" ratings they can give. "To maintain a credible profile, the senior rater must have less than 50 percent of the ratings of a rank in the "Most Qualified" top box.[15] The next level for senior raters is "Highly Qualified," and similar to raters, the HQDA will process OERs with a "Most Qualified" senior rater assessment that pushes their profile above the 50 percent threshold with an electronically generated "Highly Qualified" label.[16] This system serves to prevent evaluation report inflation. The key for a joint officer assigned to rate on Army officers is to remain aware of these criteria and manage their profiles. The OER form has verbiage in Block e that tells the rater they are limited to less than 50 percent "Excels" ratings. The OER also shows the total number of ratings the rater and senior rater have given and how many officers they currently rate in that grade (i.e. Majors, Lieutenant Colonels, Colonels). The senior rater gets one last block in Part VI where they can offer three successive assignments they deem that Soldier most suited for. In the example, the senior rater offered a map for this Major to move to Battalion Command, a key headquarters operations assignment, and a staff leadership assignment. Both the rater and senior rater can also offer a narrative comment with their overall assessment of the officer with a stratification. A lack of any numerical stratification would represent a diminished perception of that officer's performance and future potential, a top X% is better, and a #1 of XX is the best.

HQDA#: 146 786 8

NAME		SSN (or DOD ID No.)	PERIOD COVERED:	FROM (YYYYMMDD) 20160504	THRU (YYYYMMDD) 201705 03

d.2. Provide narrative comments which demonstrate performance regarding field grade competencies and attributes in the Rated Officer's current duty position. (i.e. demonstrates resilient presence, confidence and resilience in a specific duties and unexpected situation; adjusts to altered influence on the mission or taskings and organization; prioritizes a limited resources to accomplish mission, proactive in developing others through individual coaching counseling and mentoring; active learner to master organizational level knowledge, critical thinking and visioning skills, anticipates and provides for subordinates on-the-job needs for training and development; effective communicator across echelons and innovation, proficient in engaging others; presenting information and recommendations and persuasion, highly proficient at critical thinking, judgment and cohesion the Army chain of command; effective at engaging others, presenting information and recommendations and persuasion; highly proficient at critical thinking, judgment and cohesion, proficient in utilizing Army design method of and other to solve complex problems, uses all influence techniques to empower others; proactive in gaining trust in negotiations, remains respectful, firm and fair. Fully supports SHARP and create a positive command/workplace environment.)

COMMENTS:
MAJ XXX is unflappable. He is well regarded by his international colleagues with the depth of his experience and knowledge especially as we address issues with A2AD in the COE. His skills with red teaming makes him a valuable member of the HQs. He is a critical, creative and disciplined problem solver, which amplifies his energy and diligence in finding solutions and then implementing them through his own initiative.

e. This Officer's overall Performance is Rated as: (Select one box representing Rated Officer's overall performance compared to others of the same grade whom you have rated in your career. Managed at less than 50% in EXCELS.)

A completed DA Form 67-10-1A was received with this report and considered in my evaluation and review. ☒ Yes ☐ No (explain in comments below)

HQDA COMPARISON OF THE RATER'S PROFILE AND BOX CHECK AT THE TIME THIS REPORT PROCESSED

EXCELS

RO:	SSN:	IR:	SSN:
DATE: 2017-07-14	TOTAL RATINGS 14	RATINGS THIS OFFICER: 1	I currently rate **14** Army Officers in this grade.

Comments:
Outstanding performance in every respect. Clearly in the top 10% of ADA officers. A team player that gets great results. Interpersonal skills and tact coupled with remarkable organization and staff skills mark MAJ XXX as a top performer.

PART V - INTERMEDIATE RATER

PART VI - SENIOR RATER

a. POTENTIAL COMPARED WITH OFFICERS SENIOR RATED IN SAME GRADE (OVERPRINTED BY DA)	b. I currently senior rate __7__ Army Officers in this grade.
HQDA COMPARISON OF THE SENIOR RATER'S PROFILE AND BOX CHECK AT THE TIME THIS REPORT PROCESSED	c. COMMENTS ON POTENTIAL: MAJ XXX is #1 of 7 US Army Majors and is the absolute best of the hand-picked, multinational cohort of Majors in this NATO, three-star, joint headquarters at readiness. He is my first choice for below the zone promotion to LTC and tactical battalion command, where he will serve with distinction. XXX's potential is truly unlimited. A future general officer.
MOST QUALIFIED	
RO:	
SR:	
DATE: 2017-07-14	d. List 3 future SUCCESSIVE assignments for which this Officer is best suited
TOTAL RATINGS: 42	ADA Battalion Commander; AAMDC G3; AAMDC Chief of Staff
RATINGS THIS OFFICER: 1	

DA FORM 67-10-2, NOV 2015

Page 2 of 2
APD LC v1.00es

Source: LTC John Doe, "Sample Army Officer Evaluation Report"

Navy FITREP

The Navy's Bureau of Naval Personnel (BUPERS) provides guidance on how to evaluate Navy personnel through its BUPERS Instruction 1610.10E, "Navy Performance Evaluation System," dated December 6, 2019, which replaced version 1610.10D. According to the instruction, the Navy system uses a FITREP for officers, warrant officers, and senior enlisted personnel.[17] Personnel are graded on performance traits "on a 5-point scale, from 1.0 (lowest) to 5.0 (highest). A 3.0 represents performance that fully meets Navy standards, and the instruction directs that raters reserve higher grades for performance "which significantly exceeds standards."[18] Any grade of 1.0 makes the report adverse and the rater must substantiate a 1.0 rating with additional comments. Additionally, all Navy FITREPs include a five-step promotion recommendation scale: "Significant problems," "Progressing," "Promotable," "Must Promote," and "Early Promote."[19] Navy rules limit the number of "Most Promote" and "Early Promote" recommendations a Rater can give.[20]

Unlike the other services, the Navy generally follows a strict guideline on when officers receive a FITREP. According to the Navy's FITREP Periodic Reporting Calendar (Figure 10), Lieutenant Commanders (O4s) receive a report in October, Commanders (O5s) receive one in April, and Captains (O6s) receive one in July. This schedule provides a predictable schedule for all officer reports and synchronizes their personnel records with the Navy's promotion board and other selection board schedules. However, if an officer moves into or out of an assignment between report cycles, an additional report may be required to document that officer's performance during the period. The regulation states the following regarding report timing:

"A Periodic report may be omitted if a member has received a graded Regular report within the prior 3 months. The omitted period is included in the next Regular report. Otherwise, periodic reports must be submitted on the above dates [Table 1, Figure 10], and may be extended by letter for up to 3 months in lieu of a Detachment report. In no case however, should a total report period exceed 15 months."

Source: Bureau of Naval Personnel (BUPERS) Instruction 1610.10E

Figure 15: Navy Fitness Report Calendar

TOTAL FORCE FITREP/EVAL PERIODIC REPORT CALENDAR

Applies to all Active Duty (ACDU), Full Time Support (FTS), and Inactive (INACT) duty Reserve personnel.

FITREP ending dates are the last day of the month for all officers. CHIEFEVAL and enlisted EVAL ending dates are the 15th day of the month.

	PERIODIC FITREP/CHIEFEVAL/EVAL	
	Officers (All)	Enlisted (All)
Jan	O3	
Feb	O2	
Mar	W5, W4, W3	E5
Apr	O5	E9
May	O1	
Jun		E4
Jul	O6	E3, E2, E1
Aug		
Sep	W2	E8, E7
Oct	O4	
Nov		E6
Dec		

Table 1

A Periodic report may be omitted if a member has received a graded Regular report within the prior 3 months. The omitted period is included in the next Regular report. Otherwise, periodic reports must be submitted on the above dates, and may be extended by letter for up to 3 months in lieu of a Detachment report. In no case, however, should a total report period exceed 15 months.

11

Enclosure (1)

*** (Counseling is due at the six month interval between regular reporting period ending dates.) ***

Source: Bureau of Naval Personnel (BUPERS) Instruction 1610.10E

The BUPERS Instruction 1610.10E offers detailed instructions that a rater can follow when completing a Navy report. Most of the first page (Figure 16) includes basic identifying information for the member rated on, the command, duty title, and primary duties

Figure 16: Sample Navy FITREP Page 1

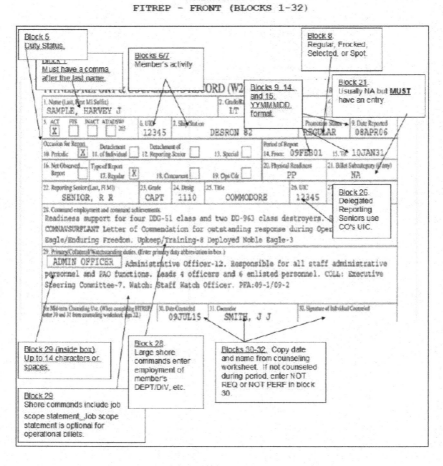

Source: Bureau of Naval Personnel (BUPERS) Instruction 1610.10E

Page 2 of the Navy FITREP (Figure 17) contains the bulk of information on the individual's performance, and this page is where the Rater will focus on the distinctions between the Navy and the other service reports. The top section allows the Rater to assess the officer based on two performance traits: Leadership and Tactical Performance on the 1.0 to 5.0 scale. In Block 40, the Rater can enter up to two career recommendations for the officer for appropriate next developmental education programs and for next assignment commensurate with the officer's pay grade aligned "for their next significant career milestone and should be useful to detailers and screening boards."[21] The Rater will enter their comments on the officer's performance in Block 42, and these comments generally follow a bullet format. The BUPERS Instruction 1610.10E offers detailed instructions in Chapter 13 on required comments, style, prohibited comments, and special interest items. Any 1.0 performance rating requires a substantiating comment, and three 2.0 performance ratings also requires comments. Raters should provide clear comments that succinctly describe the officer's performance during the reporting period.

Figure 17: Sample Navy FITREP Page 2

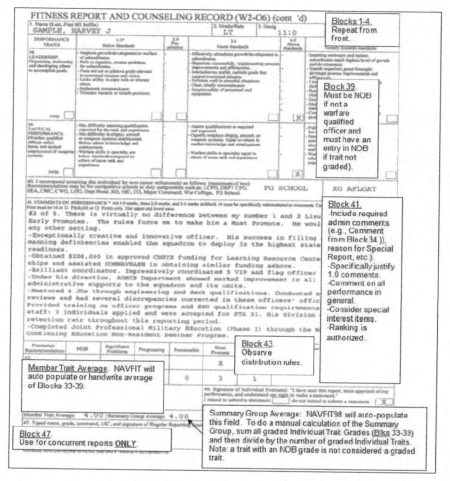

Source: Bureau of Naval Personnel (BUPERS) Instruction 1610.10E

Air Force Officer Performance Report (OPR)

Similar to the Army, the Air Force has a regulation that governs what comments can go into an Air Force officer's Air Force Form 707 known commonly as the Officer Performance Report (OPR). Air Force Instruction 36-2406, Personnel, Officer and Enlisted Evaluations Systems (AFI 36-2406). The Air Force Instruction states that, "evaluation ratings are used to document performance and potential as well as provide information for making promotion recommendation, selection, or propriety action; selective continuation; involuntary separation; selective early retirement; school nomination and selection; and other management decisions."[22] This essentially means that these annual OPRs become a permanent part of every officer's personnel record, and the Air Force uses this record for all decisions throughout an officer's career. The AFI also cautions evaluators at all levels to prevent inflation of their ratings. Unlike the Army, the Air Force does not currently use profiles for raters and additional raters, so this inflation has occurred historically.[23] The instruction also states that all officers in the rank of colonel and below require an OPR for each rating period, typically one year.

The Air Force requires an OPR on an officer when they have at least 120 calendar days of supervision, and prior to deployment when that officer is going to fill a 365-day deployment, or when there is a change in their reporting official after 120 days of supervision. Otherwise, OPRs typically follow a one-year cycle. Also, when the rater or ratee is pending separation, retirement, or permanent change in station, the close-out date of the OPR will normally be set at 30 days before the departure date.[24]

Raters will normally conduct an Initial Feedback section with their Air Force ratee within the first 60 days of the supervision period. This enables a new supervisor to meet the officer, learn about them, negotiate job responsibilities and expectations, and establish a time frame for the Mid-term feedback. Typically, the Rater will conduct a Mid-term feedback session between four and six months prior to the end of the rating period to confer with how the ratee is performing and offer opportunities for course corrections before the end of the rating period. The rater will record the date of this Mid-term feedback session and will enter it on the OPR form for date of last feedback. Raters should use the Air Force Form 724, Airman Comprehensive Assessment to conduct feedback for Air Force officers and document it, but this form never becomes part of the Air Force member's permanent personnel record. A best practice is to complete the form, meet with the Air Force member to review the form, have them sign it acknowledging the feedback, and make a copy for both the Rater and the ratee to keep. This will help in completing the OPR at the end of the rating period.

The Air Force OPR form (AF Form 707) is a two-page document. All of the Rater comments/ratings and Additional Rater comments will go on the front (Figure 18). The standard identifying information goes in the appropriate blocks, and the Duty Title and Job Description blocks will have standard verbiage to describe the duties of the officer rated on. The Air Force Instruction states that comments in bullet format are mandatory in the Job Description section and limited to four lines. Standard information will include the ratee's level of responsibility, number of people they supervise, dollar value of resources they manage, and projects they hold responsibility for. The Job Knowledge section will have six blocks where the Rater can check one of two blocks for each quality, "Meets Standards" or "Does Not meet Standards," and one of the two blocks must be marked for each.[25]

The Air Force Instruction states that comments are mandatory in Section IV, "Rater Overall Assessment" section, and that the rater "must use bullet format."[26] In stark contrast to the Army's evaluation system, the Air Force Officer Performance Report (OPR) is characterized by bullet comments, and every effort is made to fill in the white space in both the Rater's and the Additional Rater's blocks. A close look at a typical Air Force OPR shows that the Rater's block has six lines and the Additional Rater's block allows four lines. If one were to count the number of characters in an OPR bullet, they would find that each line consists of between 122 and 126 characters. Twitter allows 140 characters, so these 10 bullets on an OPR mean the Rater and Additional Rater essentially have ten Tweets to accurately characterize an Air Force officer's performance over their one year rating period. Strong bullets on an Air Force OPR will typically follow the "-Action; Result--Impact" format to make a strong line. For example, and Air Force officer is assigned to lead an Operational Planning Team to develop a new Operations Plan for the Combatant Commander. This plan significantly improves the Command's posture to deal with a particular situation. The bullet might read something like "Expertly led 15-member planning tm; crafted 120-page plan in 3 mths--approved by SECDEF, Cmd prepared for rapid response." The rater needs to condense the language to fit a lot of information onto each line to make a strong OPR for the officer.

Figure 18: Sample Air Force OPR Page 1

OFFICER PERFORMANCE REPORT *(Lt thru Col)*

I. RATEE IDENTIFICATION DATA *(Read AFI 36-2406 carefully before filling in any item)*

1. NAME *(Last, First, Middle Initial)*	2. SSN	3. RANK	4. DAFSC	5. REASON FOR REPORT	6. PAS CODE
LAST, FIRST, M.	123-45-6789	Lt Col	13S4	Annual	AB3ERTYS

7. ORGANIZATION, COMMAND, LOCATION, AND COMPONENT: Joint Planning Support Element (JPSE), Joint Capabilities Command (JECC), U.S. Transportation Command (USTRANSCOM), Norfolk, VA (AD)

8. PERIOD OF REPORT: FROM 1 Jul 2018 THRU 30 Jun 2019

9. NO. DAYS SUPV. 365 / NO. DAYS NON-RATED 0

II. JOB DESCRIPTION *(Limit text to 4 lines)*
DUTY TITLE: CHIEF, FUTURE PLANS

10. SRID: U61JT

- Leads JPSE's Special Technical Operations Cell; conducts joint deliberate/crisis planning in support of all GCCs
- Conducts planning and execution of Combatant Commander OPLANS, CONPLANS, and regional security plans
- Integrates and coordinates space, cyber, & info operations across the full spectrum of joint warfighting capabilities
- Plans/executes joint operations in accordance with JPP as a Global Response Force planner in support of GCCs

III. PERFORMANCE FACTORS

	DOES NOT MEET STANDARDS	MEETS STANDARDS
Job Knowledge, Leadership Skills (to include Promoting a Healthy Organizational Climate), Professional Qualities, Organizational Skills, Judgment and Decisions, Communication Skills (see reverse if marked Does Not Meet Standards)	☐	☒

IV. RATER OVERALL ASSESSMENT *(Limit text to 6 lines)*

- Flawlessly led 12-mbr planning team ISO biannual US-Japan jnt exer--lauded by USFJ CDR as best event in 18 yrs
- Hand-picked Dep Ex Lead for biannual US-Aus TS 15; secured 20 jnt billets--fulfilled JECC CDR's trng priorities
- Theater expert; authored/revised PACOM CDR's key plans--key player in three Tier-1 exer: KE14 / AS14 / UFG14
- Interagency expert; filled vital AS14 jnt interagency coord billet--enabled resp to notional Alaska 50-yr earthquake
- Aced 4 Jt crs's; 650 hrs continuing ed, INTAC, JIOPC, JPME II, ACQ 201B--supremely prepared to support GCCs
- #4 of 36 jnt svc O-5s in Plans; All-star planner & ldr--Grp Dpty CC next, then SDE w/follow-on JCS assignment

Last performance feedback was accomplished on: 3 Apr 2019 (IAW AFI 36-2406) *(If not accomplished, state the reason)*

NAME, GRADE, BR OF SVC, ORGN, COMMAND & LOCATION	DUTY TITLE	DATE
JOHN A. DOE, COL, USA / Joint Enabling Capabilities Command, (USTRANSCOM), Norfolk, VA 23511	Chief, Joint Planning Support Element Plans / SSN 1234 / SIGNATURE	

V. ADDITIONAL RATER OVERALL ASSESSMENT *(Limit text to 4 lines)*   ☐ CONCUR   ☐ NON-CONCUR

- Expert Air/Space planner; Supported 120-day standup of JTF for Op Inherent Resolve--took fight to ISIL enemies
- Jt Ops Coord Element Chief for UFG 14; briefed ROK, USFK J3s--vital conduit between ROK JCS & USFK CDR
- Brilliantly led 14-mbr OPT in MRX 15.1--Msn Analysis Brf/BPLAN lauded by JECC/J3 as "best seen in 9 MRXs"
- Top 10% of jnt service O-5s; always delivers A+ results--My #1 choice for SDE, OG/CD, then key JCS assignment

NAME, GRADE, BR OF SVC, ORGN, COMMAND & LOCATION	DUTY TITLE	DATE
JOHN B DOE, COL, USA / Joint Planning Support Element, (USTRANSCOM) Norfolk, VA 23511	Commander, Joint Planning Support Element / SSN 4567 / SIGNATURE	

VI. REVIEWER *(If required, limit text to 3 lines)*   ☐ CONCUR   ☐ NON-CONCUR

NAME, GRADE, BR OF SVC, ORGN, COMMAND & LOCATION	DUTY TITLE	DATE
CHESTER W. NIMITZ, RDML, USN / Joint Enabling Capabilities Command, (USTRANSCOM) Norfolk, VA 23511	Commander / SSN 6789 / SIGNATURE	

VII. FUNCTIONAL EXAMINER/AIR FORCE ADVISOR *(Indicate applicable review by marking the appropriate box)*   ☐ FUNCTIONAL EXAMINER   ☐ AIR FORCE ADVISOR

NAME, GRADE, BR OF SVC, ORGN, COMMAND & LOCATION	DUTY TITLE	DATE
HENRY H. ARNOLD, Col, USAF / Joint Enabling Capabilities Command, (USTRANSCOM) Norfolk, VA 23511	Air Force Element Commander / SSN 2345 / SIGNATURE	

VIII. RATEE'S ACKNOWLEDGMENT

I understand my signature does not constitute agreement or disagreement. I acknowledge all required feedback was accomplished during the reporting period and upon receipt of this report.   Yes ☐ No ☐   SIGNATURE ___   DATE

AF FORM 707, 20150731, V1   (PREVIOUS EDITIONS ARE OBSOLETE)   PRIVACY ACT INFORMATION: The information in this form is FOR OFFICIAL USE ONLY. Protect IAW the Privacy Act of 1974.

Source: Lt Col Ted Roberts, Sample OPR

Raters and Additional Raters typically reserve the bottom line of their respective blocks for any stratifications, push for next level of developmental education, next level of command, and for next appropriate assignment. In the example OPR (Figure 18), both the Rater and the Additional Rater provide bottom lines in their respective blocks that include this. While the Air Force Instruction doesn't define this rule, an unwritten hierarchy exists for stratifications. The strongest stratification a rater could enter would rate the officer #1/XX O-5s or whatever rank the officer is. The Rater can only rank the officer among peers within that rater's authority. In the example, the Rater had 36 O-5s (i.e. Lieutenant Colonels or Commanders) in his element, and he ranked this particular O5 officer "#4 of 36 joint service O-5s." This represents a second-tier stratification which essentially puts this officer in the Top 10%. A third-tier stratification would state "Top 10%" or "Top 15%." Finally, a fourth-tier stratification would include no numbers and simply provide an adjective such as "Outstanding officer." To officers unaccustomed to the Air Force rating system, an OPR with bottom lines filled with "Outstanding" or "Excellent" might seem really good, to Air Force board members accustomed to seeing many officer records, this represents an officer who is on track with average performance.

The Rater includes the other three elements mentioned in the bottom line, a push for next level of command appropriate for the officer, a push for appropriate next level of developmental education (Senior Developmental Education or SDE for O-5s), and a push for next assignment "key JCS assignment" which would vector this officer to a strategic-level headquarters assignment in the Pentagon. The lack of these three items in the bottom line potentially sends a less-than-positive message to selection boards considering this officer for command or school opportunities. Similarly, the Additional Rater in this example used a similar format and verbiage in his bottom line. The Commander, or in a headquarters organization, the Directorate chief (J3, J4, etc.) typically signs as the Reviewer and makes no comments. If none of the three officials in the Air Force officer's rating chain is Air Force, then a senior Air Force representative on the staff will also review the report and sign as an Air Force Advisor to provide a sanity check on the report and make sure it doesn't violate Air Force rules while also ensuring the report adequately represents the officer before going into his or her permanent personnel record.

The second page of the Air Force OPR (Figure 19) requires minimal input from the Rater. The Rater can check one of the boxes for "Does Not Meet Standards" for one of the six Performance factors, but this is atypical unless this will be an adverse Referral OPR.

Figure 19: Air Force OPR Example Page 2

RATEE NAME: LAST, FIRST, M.		
IX. PERFORMANCE FACTORS (if Section III is marked Does Not Meet Standards, fill in applicable block[s])		DOES NOT MEET STANDARDS
1. Job Knowledge. Has knowledge required to perform duties effectively. Strives to improve knowledge. Applies knowledge to handle non-routine situations.		☐
2. Leadership Skills. Sets and enforces standards. Promotes a Healthy Organizational Climate. Works well with others. Fosters teamwork. Displays initiative. Self-confident. Motivates subordinates. Has respect and confidence of subordinates. Fair and consistent in evaluation of subordinates.		☐
3. Professional Qualities. Exhibits loyalty, discipline, dedication, integrity, honesty, and officership. Adheres to Air Force Standards (i.e. Fitness standards, dress and appearance, customs and courtesies, and professional conduct.) Accepts personal responsibility, is fair and objective.		☐
4. Organizational Skills. Plans, coordinates, schedules and uses resources effectively. Meets suspenses. Schedules work for self and others equitably and effectively. Anticipates and solves problems.		☐
5. Judgment and Decisions. Makes timely and accurate decisions. Emphasizes logic in decision making. Retains composure in stressful situations. Recognizes opportunities. Adheres to safety and occupational health requirements. Acts to take advantage of opportunities.		☐
6. Communication Skills. Listens, speaks, and writes effectively.		☐

X. REMARKS (use this section to spell out acronyms from the front)

Ardent Sentry (AS); Commander (CDR); Geographic Combatant Command (GCC); Individual Terrorism Awareness Course (INTAC); Joint Operational Planning Process (JOPP); Joint Info Ops Planners' Course (JIOPC); KEEN EDGE (KE); Long Range Planning Element (LRPE); Mission Ready Exercise (MRX); Operational Plan (OPLAN); Operational Planning Team (OPT); Pacific Command (PACOM); Ready JECC Package (RJP); TALISMAN SABRE (TS); ULCHI FREEDOM GUARDIAN (UFG)

XI. REFERRAL REPORT (Complete only if report contains referral comments or the overall standards block is marked as does not meet standards)
I am referring this OPR to you according to AFI 36-2406, para 1.10. It contains comment(s)/rating(s) that make(s) the report a referral as defined in AFI 36-2406, para. 1.10.
Specifically,

Acknowledge receipt by signing and dating below. Your signature merely acknowledges that a referral report has been rendered; it does not imply acceptance of or agreement with the ratings or comments on the report. Once signed, you are entitled to a copy of this memo. You may submit rebuttal comments. Send your written comments to:

not later than 3 duty days (30 for non-EAD members) from your date below. If you need additional time, you may request an extension from the individuals named above. You may submit attachments (limit to 10 pages), but they must directly relate to the report which this report was referred. Pertinent attachments not maintained elsewhere will remain attached to the report for file in your personal record. Copies of previous reports, etc. submitted as attachments will be removed from your rebuttal package prior to filing since these documents are already filed in your records. Your rebuttal comments/attachments may not contain any reflection on the character, conduct, integrity, or motives of the evaluator unless you can fully substantiate and document them. Contact the MPS, Force Management section, or the AF Contact Center if you require any assistance in preparing your reply to the rebuttal.
It is important for you to be aware that receiving a referral report may affect your eligibility for other personnel related actions (e.g. assignments, promotions, etc.). You may consult your commander and/or MPS or Air Force Contact Center if you desire more information on this subject. If you believe this report is inaccurate, unjust, or unfairly prejudicial to your career, you may apply for a review of the report under AFI 36-2406, Chapter 10, Correction of Officer and Enlisted Evaluation Reports, once the report becomes a matter of record as defined in AFI 36-2406, Attachment 2.

NAME, GRADE, BR OF SVC OF REFERRING EVALUATOR	DUTY TITLE		DATE
	SIGNATURE		
SIGNATURE OF RATEE			DATE

INSTRUCTIONS

ALL: Recommendations must be based on performance and the potential based on that performance. Promotion recommendations are prohibited. Do not comment on completion of or enrollment in Developmental Education, advanced education, previous or anticipated promotion recommendations on AF Form 709, OPR endorsement levels, family activities, marital status, race, sex, ethnic origin, age, religion or sexual orientation. Evaluators enter only the last four numbers of SSN.

RATER: Focus your evaluation in Section IV on what the officer did, how well he or she did it, and how the officer contributed to mission accomplishment. Write in concise "bullet" format. Your comments in Section IV may include recommendations for assignment. Provide a copy of the report to the ratee prior to the report becoming a matter of record and provide follow-up feedback to let the ratee know how their performance resulted in this final product.

ADDITIONAL RATER: Carefully review the rater's evaluation to ensure it is accurate, unbiased and uninflated. If you disagree, you may ask the rater to review his or her evaluation. You may not direct a change in the evaluation. If you still disagree with the rater, mark "NON-CONCUR" and explain. You may include recommendation for assignment.

REVIEWER: Carefully review the rater's and additional rater's ratings and comments. If their evaluations are accurate, unbiased and uninflated, mark "CONCUR" and sign the form. If you disagree with previous evaluators, you may ask them to review their evaluations. You may not direct them to change their appraisals. If you still disagree with the additional rater, mark "NON-CONCUR" and explain in Section VI. Do not use "NON-CONCUR" simply to provide comments on the report.

RATEE: Your signature is merely an acknowledgement of receipt of this report. It does not constitute concurrence. If you disagree with the content, you may file an evaluation appeal through the Evaluation Reports Appeals Board IAW AFI 36-2406 Chapter 10 (Correcting Officer and Enlisted Evaluation Reports), or through the Air Force Board for Correction of Military Records IAW AFI 36-2603 (Air Force Board for Correction of Military Records) and AFPAM 36-2607 (Applicant's Guide to the Air Force Board for Correction of Military Records (AFBCMR).

PRIVACY ACT STATEMENT

AUTHORITY: Title 10 United States Code (U.S.C.) 8013, Secretary of the Air Force; AFI 36-2406, and Executive Order 0397 (SSN), as amended.
PURPOSE: Used to document effectiveness/duty performance history; promotion, school and assignment selection; reduction-in-force; control roster; reenlistment; separation; research and statistical analysis.
ROUTINE USES: May specifically be disclosed outside the DoD as a routine use pursuant to 5 U.S.C. 552a(b)(3). DoD Blanket Routine Uses apply.
DISCLOSURE: Voluntary. Not providing SSN may cause form to not be processed or to positively identify the person being evaluated.
SORN: F036 AF PC A, Effectiveness/Performance Reporting Records

AF FORM 707, 20150731, V1	(PREVIOUS EDITIONS ARE OBSOLETE)	PRIVACY ACT INFORMATION: The information in this form is FOR OFFICIAL USE ONLY. Protect IAW the Privacy Act of 1974.

Source: Lt Col Ted Roberts, Sample OPR

Marine Fitness Report

The Marine Corps Order (MCO) 1610.7A, Performance Evaluation System (PES) governs Marine Corps appraisals. The PES, dated May 1, 2018 revised "the previous policies, procedures, and standards for the operation and maintenance of the Marine Corps Performance Evaluation System (PES)" and governs fitness reports for all Marines between the rank of sergeant through major general.[27] The Marine Corps uses their fitness reports as "the primary means for evaluating a Marine's performance to support the Commandant's efforts to select the best qualified personnel for promotion, career designation, retention, resident schooling, command, and duty assignments."[28] Any officer who rates on a Marine, either as a Reporting Senior or as a Reviewing Officer, will have to establish a Marine Online account which they can do through the Marine Corps administrative office at their joint organization.

The Marines use the USMC Fitness Report (1610) (Figure 20) to conduct annual appraisals on Marines. This five-page form has detailed rules for how to properly complete it that a joint officer assigned to rate on Marines should become familiar with. Unlike the Air Force, which typically only requires OPRs annually or when the officer has a change of rating official, the Marine Corps PES requires a fitness report for any of thirteen occasions.

1. Grade change (promotion)
2. Commandant of the Marine Corps (CMC) Directed – for significant administrative, commendatory, or adverse action
3. Change of Reporting Senior
4. Transfer
5. Change of Duty
6. To Temporary Duty
7. From Temporary Duty
8. End of Service
9. Change in Status
10. Annual (Active Component)

11. Annual (Reserve Component)

12. Semiannual (Lieutenants only)

13. Reserve Training

Source: Marine Corps PES

Figure 20: Marine Corps FITREP

| USMC FITNESS REPORT (1610) NAVMC 10835 (Rev. 7-11) (EF) PREVIOUS EDITIONS WILL NOT BE USED FOUO – Privacy sensitive when filled in. | COMMANDANT'S GUIDANCE | DO NOT STAPLE THIS FORM |

The completed fitness report is the most important information component in manpower management. It is the primary means of evaluating a Marine's performance and is the Commandant's primary tool for the selection of personnel for promotion, augmentation, resident schooling, command, and duty assignments. Therefore, the completion of this report is one of an officer's most critical responsibilities. Inherent in this duty is the commitment of each Reporting Senior and Reviewing Officer to ensure the integrity of the system by giving close attention to accurate marking and timely reporting. Every officer serves a role in the scrupulous maintenance of this evaluation system, ultimately important to both the individual and the Marine Corps. Inflationary markings only serve to dilute the actual value of each report. Reviewing Officers will not concur with inflated reports.

Source: US Marine Corps Form 1610, "Marine Corps Fitness Report"

Block A: Administrative Information in the Marine Fitness Report consists primarily of the Marine's identifying information, unit description, and the period observed. However, this block also contains blocks for the Marine's Personal Fitness Test results, Combat Fitness Test results, shooting qualifications, as well as identification of the Marine's rater (Reporting Senior) and additional rater (Reviewing Officer). Finally, Block 7 allows the Reviewing Officer to make a promotion recommendation. Typically, the raters check the "Yes" block. If the "No" block is checked, then the Marine Corps will consider this an "Adverse" fitness report and will negatively impact the Marine's career and potential for further advancement.

Blocks B and C provide space to describe the Marine Rated On's (MRO's) billet and assigned duties and the MRO's most significant accomplishments during the year in that billet. Reporting Seniors typically use a bullet format to fill in these blocks, and seek to fill all the lines with the description and accomplishments. The Marine and their Reporting Senior will meet at the beginning of the rating period to negotiate the billet description during initial counseling so the Marine knows their assigned duties and performance expectations. The MRO and the Rating Senior will complete the Marine Rated On Worksheet (MROW) to confer and agree on the billet description. At the end of the rating period, the Reporting Senior will complete Section C, the Billet Accomplishments section. The PES directs Reporting Seniors to restrict the Section C comments to only the space provided, use bulletized text format, and "precede each entry by a distinctive mark (e.g. a circle or dash)."[29]

Pages two through four of the Marine FITREP (Figure 21) contain the 14 attributes for the Reporting Senior to rate the Marine on. According to the PES, "the fitness report describes the 'whole Marine' both on and off duty," and "this picture goes beyond the MRO's assigned duties (section B) and what the Marine accomplished (section C); it also records the manner in which the Marine discharged those duties and responsibilities."[30] Accordingly, sections D, E, F, G, and H include 14 attributes to "evaluate the MRO that the Marine Corps deems most important" across a broad cross-section.[31] The scale (known as a Performance-Anchored Rating Scale or PARS) for each of the 14 attributes runs from A to H. An "A" rating reflects an adverse rating and would require an additional justification comment at the bottom of that section. Most Marines receive a rating between B and D, with a "B" equating to below average, a "C" as average, and a "D" as above average. An "E" rating is far above average and rare. "F" and "G" ratings represent extremely high ratings and are therefore extremely rare. Any Reporting Senior who rates a Marine an "F" or a "G" rating must provide a written justification to support that rating. The impact of this system is that justification statements are very rare under the 14 attributes. If a reader sees a comment in the justification section, this will flag them to read it and look for an "A" adverse rating or a very rare "F" or "G" rating for unusually exceptional performance.

Figure 21: Marine FITREP Pages 2-4

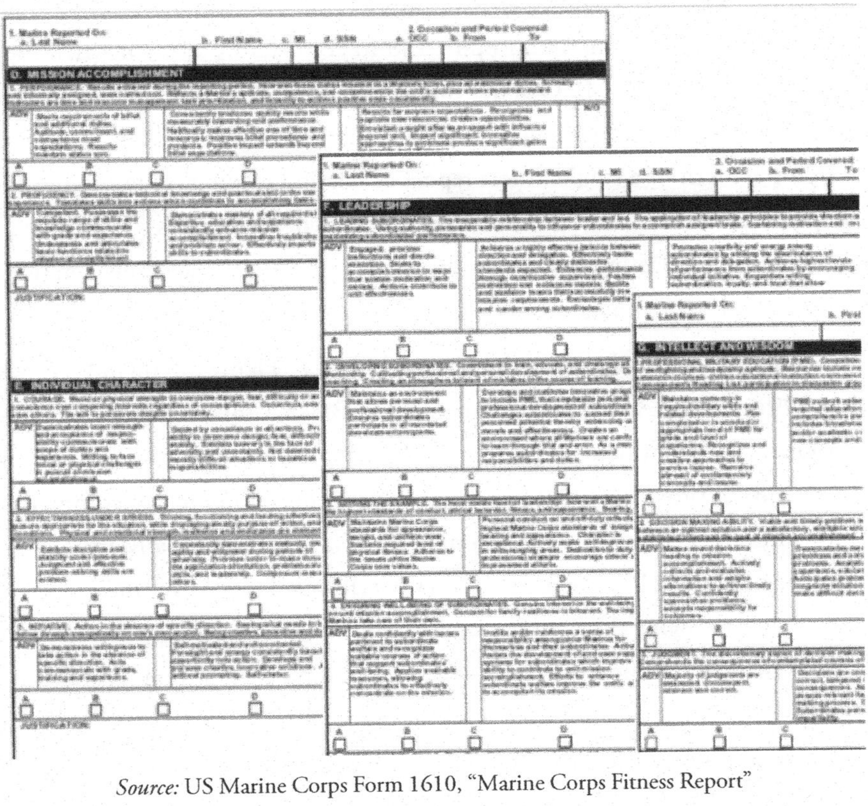

Source: US Marine Corps Form 1610, "Marine Corps Fitness Report"

Reporting Seniors need to develop a "Marking Philosophy" when they begin conducting appraisals for Marines.[32] The Marine Corps also has a system for negating grade inflation on its FITREPs. Reporting Seniors build a profile for their ratings over time based on the number of Marines they rate and the historical trends for the ratings they give. Once a Reporting Senior (RS) has rated on three Marines in the same grade, they have established a profile which tracks their averages. The MCO states that "A marking philosophy refers to the weight a RS assigns to the PARS for individual attributes. Reporting Seniors need to develop a consistent marking philosophy so that the Marines they rate in their profile have a consistent standard. Once a Reporting Senior has rated at least three Marines, the automated system will calculate a Relative Value (RV) for their ratings. The lowest Marine gets an 80, the highest-rated Marine gets a 100, and the receive a score between those two. The important consideration for joint officers rating on Marines for the first time is to realize the importance of developing a marking philosophy, and to consistently apply it when they rate on Marines. The MCO states that the Relative value's principal purpose is "to give individuals making personnel management decisions the ability to weigh the merit of a single fitness report in relation to the RS's rating history or 'profile.'"[33] This means giving excessively high or low ratings to a particular Marine will not overly skew the results when that Marine faces considerations for promotion, command, or developmental education.

The fifth and final page of the Marine FITREP (Figure 22) includes Block I for Directed and Additional comments, and Block K for the Reviewing Officer rating and comments. The Reporting Senior must enter any mandatory comments to provide a fuller picture of the Marine, and Directed comments, and Additional comments. An example for this might be for a Marine in an elite unit. Marine Helicopter Squadron One (HMX-1) is the Marine squadron responsible for flying the President and Vice President. As a highly elite unit, all Marine helicopter pilots are hand-selected based on their strong record to fly for this unit. A Reporting Senior could add a comment to a Marine's FITREP that they're assigned to this elite unit which is filled with the best helicopter pilots in the service. An average rating or even slightly below average rating for a

Marine assigned to this unit would seem potentially detrimental to their career. Section I gives the Rating Senior the opportunity to offer comments to "give the CMC (Commandant of the Marine Corps) a more complete picture of the MRO's professional character, performance, and potential which are not readily apparent from the attribute marks or other narrative portions of the report."[34]

Figure 22: Marine FITREP Page 5

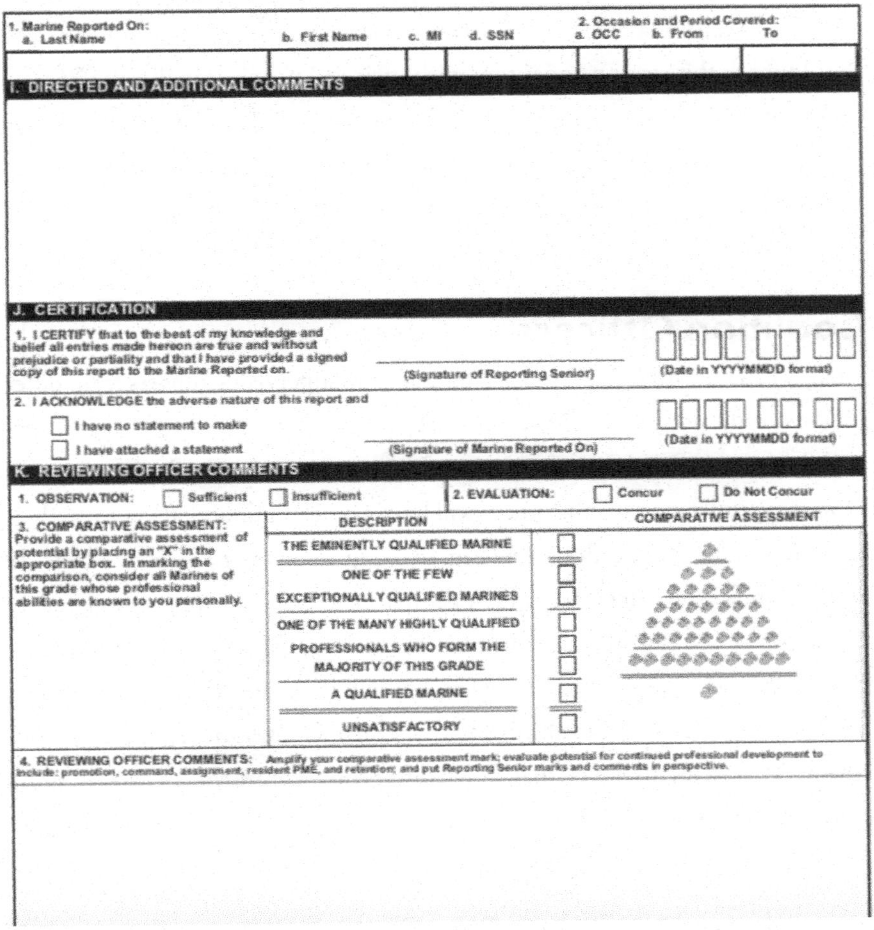

1. Marine Reported On:
a. Last Name | b. First Name | c. MI | d. SSN
2. Occasion and Period Covered:
a. OCC | b. From | To

I. DIRECTED AND ADDITIONAL COMMENTS

J. CERTIFICATION

1. I CERTIFY that to the best of my knowledge and belief all entries made hereon are true and without prejudice or partiality and that I have provided a signed copy of this report to the Marine Reported on.
(Signature of Reporting Senior)
(Date in YYYYMMDD format)

2. I ACKNOWLEDGE the adverse nature of this report and
☐ I have no statement to make
☐ I have attached a statement
(Signature of Marine Reported On)
(Date in YYYYMMDD format)

K. REVIEWING OFFICER COMMENTS

1. OBSERVATION: ☐ Sufficient ☐ Insufficient
2. EVALUATION: ☐ Concur ☐ Do Not Concur

3. COMPARATIVE ASSESSMENT: Provide a comparative assessment of potential by placing an "X" in the appropriate box. In marking the comparison, consider all Marines of this grade whose professional abilities are known to you personally.

DESCRIPTION | COMPARATIVE ASSESSMENT

THE EMINENTLY QUALIFIED MARINE
ONE OF THE FEW EXCEPTIONALLY QUALIFIED MARINES
ONE OF THE MANY HIGHLY QUALIFIED PROFESSIONALS WHO FORM THE MAJORITY OF THIS GRADE
A QUALIFIED MARINE
UNSATISFACTORY

4. REVIEWING OFFICER COMMENTS: Amplify your comparative assessment mark; evaluate potential for continued professional development to include: promotion, command, assignment, resident PME, and retention; and put Reporting Senior marks and comments in perspective.

Source: US Marine Corps Form 1610, "Marine Corps Fitness Report"

Finally, the Reviewing Officer (RO) uses Block K to provide their concurrence or non-concurrence, and rating of the Marine. Similar to the Reporting Senior, the Reviewing Officer has a profile based on historical ratings given. The

"Christmas Tree" in the comparative assessment section illustrates where the Reviewing Officer would rate this Marine relative to all others, and they check one of the eight boxes in this section. Similar to the Reporting Senior's ratings in the 14 attributes, nearly all ratings given by Reviewing Officers fall within the three blocks next to the broadest part of the tree. Checking the block next to the "A Qualified Marine" is an adverse rating and rare. Checking any boxes next to "Exceptionally Qualified Marines" or higher is also rare, and the RO should mark this section consistent with their RO profile. Finally, the RO can make amplifying comments in the box below to talk about that Marine's future potential. The RO can make recommendations for promotion to the next grade, next level of developmental education, and push for their next job or next level of command. RO comments can be narrative or in bulletized format.

Coalition Officers

Finally, you may find yourself working with and supervising officers from other nations. Typically, you will have minimal involvement with completing performance reports or decoration citations for international officers. The way this process typically works is the officer will have a senior military officer from their nation either in the headquarters organization or at their respective Defense Attaché's office at their embassy in Washington, DC. This senior representative may contact you and request some inputs for that officer's accomplishments over the previous year. A best practice is to talk with the officer you supervise and agree on what accomplishments they performed over the reporting period, ensure the statements are factual, and submit those comments to their nation's senior service representative. That representative will incorporate those inputs into the officer's annual report that will go into their personnel record. This process will ensure you have some influence as the rating official, but also ensures that international officer has the correct format and appropriate verbiage to account for their time working in a United States-led headquarters organization. Each country also has particular rules for awarding U.S. military decorations to their officers. While very important for U.S. officers, these decorations and accompanying citations may not be allowed in the personnel records for those international officers. It falls on that nation's senior military service representative to make that determination.

Final Thoughts on Evaluations

Each service has very different rating systems and timelines for their officers. An officer assigned to a joint organization and placed in a situation where they must rate officers from other services can find learning these different systems and forms overwhelming. Gaining familiarity with the report formats and the rules for completing them will prove vital to success in a joint organization. Many officers just turn this over to the ratees and allow them to complete the forms in accordance with their respective services' guidance. However, the Rater must ensure they have an input that accurately reflects the officer's performance while on the joint staff. This really becomes a balancing act to both ensure the officer is taken care of and does not face detrimental career impacts when they return to their service, but also ensuring that every officer doesn't walk away with inflated reports that dilute the evaluation systems. An individual arriving in a joint organization and assigned to evaluate officers should make it a point to meet with each of them individually at the beginning to establish clear communications, agree on performance expectations, and set a positive tone. Develop a battle rhythm to know when evaluatees will require a report, and ensure that you conduct a performance feedback session with them to discuss their objectives and accomplishments so both you and the member have a mutual understanding about the ratings and comments that will go into their respective performance reports.

1   Department of the Army. Army Regulation 623-3, *Personnel Evaluation: Evaluation Reporting System*, (Washington DC: Department of the Army, June 14, 2019), 18

2   Army Regulation 623-3, *Personnel Evaluation: Evaluation Reporting System*, 18

3   Army Regulation 623-3, *Personnel Evaluation: Evaluation Reporting System*, 19.

4   Army Regulation 623-3, *Personnel Evaluation: Evaluation Reporting System*, 19.

5   Army Regulation 623-3, *Personnel Evaluation: Evaluation Reporting System*, 20.

6   Army Regulation 623-3, *Personnel Evaluation: Evaluation Reporting System*, 20.

7   Army Regulation 623-3, *Personnel Evaluation: Evaluation Reporting System*, 20.

8   Army Regulation 623-3, *Personnel Evaluation: Evaluation Reporting System*, 20.

9   Army Regulation 623-3, *Personnel Evaluation: Evaluation Reporting System*, 21.

10   Army Regulation 623-3, *Personnel Evaluation: Evaluation Reporting System*, 57.

11   Army Regulation 623-3, *Personnel Evaluation: Evaluation Reporting System*, 57.

12   Army Regulation 623-3, *Personnel Evaluation: Evaluation Reporting System*, 57.

13   Army Regulation 623-3, *Personnel Evaluation: Evaluation Reporting System*, 38.

14   Army Regulation 623-3, *Personnel Evaluation: Evaluation Reporting System*, 38.

15   Army Regulation 623-3, *Personnel Evaluation: Evaluation Reporting System*, 42.

16   Army Regulation 623-3, *Personnel Evaluation: Evaluation Reporting System*, 42.

17   Bureau of Navy Personnel (BUPERS) Instruction 1610.10E. December 6, 2019, 2

18   BUPERS Instruction 1610.10E, 2

19   BUPERS Instruction 1610.10E, 2

20   BUPERS Instruction 1610.10E, 2

21   BUPERS Instruction 1610.10E, 1-17.

22   Secretary of the Air Force. Air Force Instruction 36-2406, *Personnel, Officer and Enlisted Evaluation Systems*. November 14, 2019. Washington, DC., 69.

23   Air Force Instruction 36-2406, 69.

24   Air Force Instruction 36-2406, 72.

25   Air Force Instruction 36-2406, 89.

26   Air Force Instruction 36-2406, 89.

27   Headquarters United States Marine Corps, Marine Corps Order 1610.7A, *Performance Evaluation System*, (Washington, DC: Department of the Navy, May 1, 2018), 1.

28   Marine Corps Order 1610.7A, *Performance Evaluation System*, 2.

29   Marine Corps Order 1610.7A, *Performance Evaluation System*, 4–21.

30   Marine Corps Order 1610.7A, *Performance Evaluation System*, 4–22.

31   Marine Corps Order 1610.7A. *Performance Evaluation System*, pg.4–23.

32   Interview with LtCol Jon Stofka, USMC, Jan 31, 2020.

33   Marine Corps Order 1610.7A, *Performance Evaluation System*, 8–5.

34   Marine Corps Order 1610.7A, *Performance Evaluation System*, 4–41.

CHAPTER 9:
How to Succeed as a Leader in a Joint Environment

When military officers swear their oath of office, they make a solemn promise to support and defend the Constitution of the United States against all enemies, foreign and domestic. Unspoken during this oath rests the understanding that all officers will lead others. As Northouse stated, leadership is a process. Officers fill leadership positions, but it takes an active interest in leading and developing others to successfully lead them. A major component of leadership is building relationships and trust with those followers you will lead. These relationships and the trust form the foundation of successful leadership. It can take significant time and effort to establish trust, but only a bad moment to destroy it. By establishing this trust in followers, the leader can accomplish this process to influence a group of individuals to achieve a common goal. This second part of Northouse's leadership definition contains two key components: influence and common goals. Joint leaders seeking to influence other officers must use effective communications and need to clearly establish and communicate the common goals. Part of these common goals will come from the top of the joint or combined organization. However, the joint leader can establish subordinate goals for the division, branch, or planning team they lead that support the higher organizational goals. Engaging followers to gain their input to develop those goals and getting their buy-in will aid in ensuring they understand and will support the group and the organization to achieve those goals.

Officers assigned to lead in a joint organization need to understand that many cultures combine to influence the personnel assigned to them. Each officer comes from one of the services. Each international officer comes with their own national culture and a country-influenced Service culture. Even officers from the same Service will in many instances bring a unique experience and subculture that influences their perspectives and how they view the world and organizational problems. These diverse cultural perspectives can only enhance the organization and make it more prepared to identify and solve complex problems or react to change. An effective joint leader will actively seek to learn about the different Services, subcultures within those Services, and other countries from international officers. By striking up open conversations and demonstrating a sincere interest in other, the joint leader will progress both in knowledge as well as build those relationships and trust that will prove vital during the inevitable stressful times when the organization will have to pull together and rapidly plan for a contingency or crisis.

While leading these officers from other Services or nations, carrying a servant leader perspective and viewing oneself as a steward called to care for and prepare these officers will establish a positive mindset for your role as a joint leader. General George Patton famously stated, "Never tell people how to do things. Tell them what to do and they will surprise you with their ingenuity." Similarly, applying a Supporting or Delegating situational leadership style in a joint headquarters organization filled with seasoned professionals who have already succeeded in their respective military Services will work well to accomplish the mission. James Mattis, former Marine General and Secretary of Defense, recounted his experience leading at three levels –tactical, executive, and strategic. A great lesson he learned in leadership came from his experience as a junior officer appointed to command a recruiting platoon. He made a striking point that "if you as the commander define the mission as your responsibility, you have already failed It was *our* mission, never *my* mission."[1] Mattis stated that despite the common use of the phrase "Command and control," he instead employed the concept of "command and feedback."[2] Like Patton, Mattis believed that rather than try to control subordinates' every move, the leader should clearly state their intent and unleash their initiative.[3] This method worked well for Jim Mattis throughout his long and distinguished Marine career, and it was one he learned early on. Mattis, a renowned avid reader and student of history, cited how George Washington led the revolutionary army using a "listen, learn, and help, then lead," sequence.[4] Mattis concluded that method worked for Washington, and he found it worked for him to. An officer preparing to lead in a joint or combined organization can take this lesson to heart and use it to succeed when leading joint and coalition officers as well.

Regarding stewardship, the Services essentially lend their most precious resource, their people to the joint organizations for a joint tour. It is incumbent on the joint leader supervising these professionals to employ them effectively, lead and mentor them, but make sure they return to their respective Service better than when they left. These officers will gain a wealth of information and experience working with other services and learning more about how they and their Service fits into the big picture. They will learn about strategy formulation at the national and theater strategic levels, and they will learn how the joint force develops, exercises, and occasionally executes operational level plans. This understanding will help them when they return to their Service and lead Soldiers, Sailors, Airmen, or Marines at the tactical and operational levels. This broadened perspective will help prepare these officers for their future roles as senior leaders too.

Joint leaders also need to set personal goals and invest time into developing themselves personally and professionally. Each service publishes a professional reading list each year to its cadre of professionals to encourage them to think and prepare for their roles as leaders. Mattis is renowned for his voracious appetite for reading, and a 2018 CNBC article discussed his views on reading and his personal collection of 7,000 books.[5] Mattis held the view that "there was nothing new under the sun" and that we can always learn about virtually any situation we face by reading what others in history went through.[6] Mattis stated that he has "never been caught flat-footed by any situation, never at a loss for how any problem has been addressed before," and that while reading history hasn't always provided an answer, "it lights what is often a dark path ahead."[7] The lesson here for officers going to a joint duty assignment is to read what they can about leading in new situations, leading change, and read up on the history and current situation for the joint/combined organization they will serve in. They can also read up on joint doctrine and study strategic guidance documents to ensure they have the requisite familiarity with them before they have to dive in to a joint planning effort. Even reading historical fiction can offer strong lessons for professional leaders.

John Kelly, another former Marine general and former White House Chief of Staff reinforced Mattis's point. Kelly recounted how a mentor talked to him early in his career about the importance of professional reading. Kelly's mentor emphasized that real professionals, across all professions, read and study their professions.[8] A great doctor will read peer articles and keep up on developments in the medical field. When Admiral James Stavridis prepared his book, "The Leader's Bookshelf," John Kelly offered C.S. Forester's book, *The General* for his reading recommendation. "The General" tells the story of an officer named Curzon who starts out in one of the elite British units prior to World War I. Curzon rises through the ranks as an exemplary officer, but one who rarely reads or prepares himself intellectually for the changes in the nature of warfare. By the time of World War I, Curzon has risen to a very senior level, but due to his lack of professional preparation, he is unprepared to deal with an overwhelming German attack.[9] Kelly derived clear lessons from *The General*, among them, "leaders must keep up with the times, educate themselves, be ready to innovate, and care for their subordinates enough to think through how to succeed when old methods are clearly failing."[10]

Learning about the sister Services and getting to know and work with officers from those services is one of the best results from officers serving in joint duty assignments. This joint acculturation will happen naturally over time, but if the only interaction officers have occurs in their work environment, it will happen more slowly. A joint leader can facilitate additional acculturation by encouraging activities to mentor and having officers share their experiences outside of the mundane day-to-day staff work. For example, having Marines brief the organization on their Service and explain how the Marines rate officers will help members from the other services understand the Marine Corps and its processes better. Having an individual who has unique expertise in a particular region or with a particular mission set (e.g., Space or Cyber) present on that topic can also help broaden understanding and accelerate the acculturation process. The leader can even seek regular opportunities to get the personnel out of the office on a recurring basis (monthly or quarterly) to allow the members to socialize in a non-duty environment. The leader will have to gauge what will work based on the location and the organization, but at the Joint Forces Staff College's JPME II classes, much of the acculturation comes during intramural sports or the seminars doing off site events such as visiting historical sites the Yorktown Battlefield or the MacArthur Memorial Museum, or social activities such as dinners or other recreational activities. It's easy to get bogged down in the daily routine of staff work or planning, so sometimes a change of venue and activity can boost morale and encourage more shared understanding between officers from different services and nations.

1   James Mattis and Bing West, *Call Sign Chaos: Learning to Lead* (New York: Random House, 2019), 16.

2   Mattis and West, *Call Sign* Chaos, 17.

3   Mattis and West, *Call Sign* Chaos, 17

4   Mattis and West, *Call Sign* Chaos, 17.

5   Amanda Macias. "The Extraordinary Reading Habits of Secretary of Defense James Mattis." *CNBC*, September 15, 2018, https://www.cnbc.com/2018/09/13/defense-secretary-james-mattis-extraordinary-reading-habits.html

6   Mattis and West, *Call Sign* Chaos, XIII.

7   Macias, "Extraordinary Reading Habits."

8   James Stavridis and R. Manning Ancell, *The Leader's Bookshelf* (Annapolis Maryland: Naval Institute Press, 2017), 196

9   Stavridis and Ancell, *Leader's Bookshelf,* 196.

10 Stavridis and Ancell, *Leader's Bookshelf,* 199.

CONCLUSION

Assignment to a joint or combined organization and working in the Joint, Interagency, Intergovernmental, and Multinational (JIIM) environment brings lots of excitement, but also fear of the unknown. Most officers going to a joint organization will experience military life outside their respective service for the first time during this assignment. They will likely hold assumptions and preconceived notions of what joint life will involve and how working with and for officers from other services will seem. The best preparation is to keep an open mind, be yourself, have a willingness to learn from personnel from other services, agencies, and nations, and to maintain open lines of communication to enable conversation and relationship building. Stereotypes and preconceived notions of officers from other services and other nations, and of people from other agencies or organizations often serve as barriers to effective cooperation and communication rather than aids.

Officers from other services are great American people who may come from a small town near you or a big city on the opposite side of the country. However, all have made the voluntarily choice to serve the country and contribute in one of the services. The fact that they have attained field grade rank and been selected by their service to represent it in a joint assignment proves they have succeeded before and will likely continue to succeed away from their home service branch. Nearly all will prove themselves highly capable and highly educated, which makes them well prepared for the dynamic joint and combined environment. In many cases, these officers may have worked with military personnel from other countries at the tactical level through International Military Education & Training (IMET) exchange programs.

Officers frequently go to a joint or combined assignment with minimal preparation. While JPME II offers a great opportunity to interact and acculturate with officers from other services or nations, and it gives a great education on the national to theater strategy-making processes and the Joint Planning Process, most officers don't get the opportunity to attend JPME until after the midpoint in their joint tour. Some don't receive it until near the end of their joint assignment if at all. A relatively small number of senior officers get to attend one of the senior service school war colleges in residence, and they receive JPME II credit for this experience, but the time spent learning about joint and combined is much more limited. Also, there is minimal time if any devoted to learning how to supervise and lead personnel from other services and nations.

This book seeks to fill that gap. An officer learning they will go to a joint assignment will have many questions. What should they know? What should they read? How can they prepare themselves to lead and succeed? This book seeks to fill that gap and provide answers to those questions. An officer reading this book will have a much better understanding of what it means to work in a joint or combined environment. They will understand some of the history behind why the U.S. military emphasizes and values joint time. They will gain a basic understanding of the national strategy-making process, how this process forms the foundation for Combatant Command and theater strategies, and how the joint force applies the doctrinal Joint Planning Process (JPP) to define problems and develop thorough solutions. Finally, the reader will gain significant insights into how to manage talent in a joint organization and the different appraisal systems for officers from different services. Many officers like a checklist for how to prepare and recommendations for readings they can dig into to further prepare. Some initial thoughts on those are offered below.

The following checklist proposes a **starting point** for officers assigned to a joint/combined organization to prepare and succeed in their new environment.

Checklist

_ Learn the staff processes for the joint/combined organization and follow them

_ Read materials to become an expert in that joint organization's area of responsibility (AOR). (e.g. For Indo-PACOM, learn about key nations in the region like China, Japan, and Korea, and international organizations like ASEAN)

_ Initiate conversations with colleagues from other services and nations

_ Build on those professional relationships with colleagues

_ Familiarize yourself with the Strategy-making processes and Joint Planning Process by reading the joint doctrine

_ Schedule initial performance feedback with supervisors to establish clear expectations and standards

_ Schedule initial performance feedback sessions with personnel you supervise to learn about them and set expectations

_ Represent your Service as an expert in that branch's warfighting domain.

Recommended further readings

- DoD Dictionary of Military and Associated Terms
- National Security Strategy (NSS)
- National Defense Strategy (NDS)
- National Military Strategy (NMS) Unclassified Summary
- Joint Strategic Campaign Plan (JSCP)
- Chairman of the Joint Chiefs Instruction 3100.01D: Joint Strategic Planning System
- Joint Publication 1: Doctrine for the Armed Forces of the United States
- Joint Publication 3-0: Joint Operations
- Joint Publication 5-0: Joint Planning

- Army Regulation 623-3: Personnel Evaluation: Evaluation Reporting System
- Air Force Instruction 36-2406 Officer and Enlisted Evaluation Systems
- Navy Bureau of Navy Personnel (BUPERS) Instruction 1610.10E
- Marine Corps Order 1610.07A: Performance Evaluation System
- *The Leaders Bookshelf* by Admiral James Stavridis
- *Call Sign Chaos: Learning to Lead* by Jim Mattis
- *A Passion for Leadership* by Robert M. Gates

ABOUT THE AUTHOR

Ted Roberts is a retired Air Force Lieutenant Colonel with more than 30 years of service. He began his Air Force career as an enlisted Airman. After three years of enlisted service, entered the United States Air Force Academy. He graduated, earned his commission and served as a career Space Operations officer. During his officer career, he graduated from the Space Weapons Instructor Course at the US Air Force Weapons School. He also has extensive Joint planning and operations experience, working as a Joint Planner supporting US Indo-Pacific Command, US Central Command, and US Transportation Command. He concluded his career as an Assistant Professor teaching Joint Planning and Joint Professional Military Education Level II (JPME II) at the Joint Forces Staff College in Norfolk, Virginia. He is a graduate of the United States Air Force Academy, and most recently graduated from Regent University with his Doctorate in Strategic Leadership in May 2020. He is married and has three children, and currently resides in Chesapeake, Virginia.